STAFF EDUCATION CENTRE
LIBRARY, RAMPTON HOSPITAL

D1758147

Hostage

Recent Titles in Contributions in Psychology

Hostage

TERROR AND TRIUMPH

James F. Campbell

CONTRIBUTIONS IN PSYCHOLOGY, NUMBER 19
Paul Pederson, *Series Adviser*

GREENWOOD PRESS
Westport, Connecticut • London

Library of Congress Cataloging-in-Publication Data

Campbell, James F.
    Hostage : terror and triumph / James F. Campbell.
        p.   cm.—(Contributions in psychology, ISSN 0736-2714 ; no.
  19)
    Includes bibliographical references and index.
    ISBN 0–313–28486–5 (alk. paper)
    1. Prison riots—New York (State) 2. Hostages—New York (State)—
  Mental health. 3. Correctional personnel—New York (State)—Mental
  health. I. Title. II. Series.
  HV9475.N7C36 1992
  365′.641—dc20   92–14354

British Library Cataloguing in Publication Data is available.

Copyright © 1992 by James F. Campbell

All rights reserved. No portion of this book may be reproduced,
by any process or technique, without the express written consent
of the publisher.

Library of Congress Catalog Card Number: 92–14354
ISBN: 0–313–28486–5
ISSN: 0736–2714

First published in 1992

Greenwood Press, 88 Post Road West, Westport, CT 06881
An imprint of Greenwood Publishing Group, Inc.

Printed in the United States of America

The paper used in this book complies with the Permanent Paper
Standard issued by the National Information Standards
Organization (Z39.48—1984).

10 9 8 7 6 5 4 3 2 1

To Susanne,
For her patience, wisdom and love,
And to Eileen, Kathleen and Peter,
For keeping me mindful of the really important
things in life.

Let's put it this way. I think once you consider yourself dead and you get a second chance, you look at things a bit differently.

Hostage Survivor

Contents

Acknowledgments

This research was born out of casual conversations with certain men at the training academy of the New York State Department of Correctional Services. While consulting there, I heard intriguing stories of remarkable events. The stories were of captivity, terror and courage. I wanted to understand better how the survivors dealt with those events through the years. This research would not have been possible without such survivors around New York State who generously agreed to be interviewed. Their stories told of the power of the human spirit to prevail over terrible adversity. They have my admiration and deep appreciation.

I am also grateful to many others for their encouragement and guidance with this project: Sari Biklen, Frances-Dee Burlin, Arnold Goldstein, Gene Knott, John Mattoon, Marshall Segal, Mary and Ed Wehying and especially Paul Pedersen. I am grateful to my editor, Paul Macirowski for his enthusiasm and confidence in this project from the moment he became involved. A special note of thanks goes to Gail Teachout, for her word processing skills and care with hundreds of pages of transcripts and manuscripts. It is unlikely this project would have reached publication without her patience and dedication.

Introduction

This is a retrospective study examining the experience of being taken hostage and the subsequent recovery process, from the point of view of the hostage survivors. The research extends the growing body of literature on victims of psychological trauma. The study focused on a specific population of hostages: twelve correction officers who were taken hostage during prison riots. Subjects, therefore, were all male and between the ages of 28 and 62. The study concentrated on long-term perspectives; most subjects were involved in prison riots in New York State during 1970 (Auburn) and 1971 (Attica). The most recent riot was in 1983 in Sing-Sing.

This study utilized a qualitative research methodology and employed in-depth interviews to gather data. Interview questions elicited views of a hostage-taking incident and subsequent experiences along fairly broad dimensions. The interviews were conducted in a manner to permit flexibility and give respondents opportunities to introduce relevant issues from their own perspectives. This was deemed appropriate to the study's exploratory purpose and its phenomenological focus. Coded interview transcripts and other field notes were used for analysis.

The men who participated in this study spoke with remarkable eloquence and power. Their interview comments that are transcribed here were not subjected to editing for grammar or style. Their names have been changed to protect their privacy.

Subjects reported that they were deeply affected by their experiences as hostages. They suffered a range of symptoms that they related to their trauma: anxiety, depression, sleep disturbances, irritability and relationship problems. While most symptoms subsided over time, the hostage survivors experienced an enduring anger at prison and state officials. This was, for some, associated with a continuing mistrust and suspicion for correctional authorities. Feelings of helplessness, a loss of a sense of competence, and a fear of annihilation were seen as major factors in the impact of the experiences.

The men acknowledged some changes in the way they viewed themselves and their world. This particular group of survivors, all of whom had returned to correctional service, also perceived some beneficial effects of their captivity experiences. They reported feeling more empathy for the suffering of others, more of a commitment to important relationships, greater confidence in their ability to overcome adversity and a desire to live their lives more fully.

Implications for the mental health profession are considered and recommendations for meeting the counseling needs of victims are offered. These recommendations include: recognizing individual differences in perception and coping with trauma, "normalizing" the victim recovery process with information and education, providing outreach services to victims as early as possible, working with and encouraging natural support systems, and providing for long-term follow-up and access to services.

This book should contribute to a growing literature on victims of violence and trauma and enhance our understanding of the way in which victims redefine and give new meaning to themselves and their world. One of the more unique aspects of the research is its long-term perspective. Few studies examine the ramifications of victimization years or decades later. With its qualitative approach, it goes deeper than the reporting of the frequency or incidences of symptoms. Further, although not a study of terrorism as such, it raises questions for future research on hostage victims in various settings.

1

Victimization: Setting the Stage

There is currently a growing concern in the mental health field regarding the mental health consequences of person-to-person victimization. This concern has been prompted by an increasing awareness of the often similar needs and problems of such diverse groups as Vietnam veterans, former prisoners of war, concentration camp survivors, kidnapping or hostage victims, and victims of rape, assault or street crime.

Victims of violent crime make up the largest of these groups. Data from the National Crime Survey (U.S. Department of Justice, 1979) indicated that 5.9 million such victimizations occurred in 1978 alone. So-called non-violent crimes like burglary and auto theft occur at rates four to five times that of violent crimes. Even non-violent offenses, however, may be experienced as a threat to one's safety and may induce a heightened sense of vulnerability. Whether it is actually violent or not, the experience of violation against the self may occur, and after-effects of the trauma may be quite similar (Bard & Sangrey, 1986).

Bard and Sangrey considered the response to victimization to be a post-traumatic stress disorder that intensifies feelings of personal helplessness and vulnerability, leading to a change in self-concept and a loss of self-esteem. Salasin (1981) further suggested that humiliation, shame and powerlessness, reinforced by social withdrawal, project an image of the self as helpless and weak. She proposed a counseling intervention to alleviate feelings of guilt, while developing mechanisms for dealing with the pain and anger. Re-establishment of a positive self-image, it was suggested, may then be possible. However, it is not clear how survivors perceive the victimization experience and how they integrate it into their lives.

THE NEED TO UNDERSTAND

Despite the profound mental health consequences for victims and their families and the limited data base in this area (Chelimisky, 1980; Everstine & Everstine, 1983; Rich & Stenzel, 1980), society and the counseling profession used to do little to identify and reach out to victims of personal violence (Sharfstein, 1980; Symonds, 1980). Counselors and psychologists in schools, clinics, hospitals, law enforcement agencies and elsewhere increasingly find themselves working with victims of sexual abuse, assault, robbery and abduction. Our fund of knowledge to help these counselors identify and meet the special needs of this population is growing, but it is still quite limited.

The depth and severity of one's emotional reaction to victimization is often a surprise to both victims and helpers. They are both members of a society that has been more inclined to attend to the exploits of criminals and police. Our culture makes television specials and best-selling books about mass murder and sensational robberies. The activities of police and criminals figure prominently in media reports; victims usually get little attention. This is particularly true if the victims did not suffer some serious physical injury. The subjective experience of victims, however, may be a profound one.

> The actual victims of real personal crime often suffer griev-
> ous and painful injuries that are not physical. They may lose
> their capacity to trust people, for example; they may be
> overwhelmed with guilt and shame; their relations with loved
> ones may suffer serious disruptions. These invisible wounds
> are rarely part of the media portrait of crime, and people tend
> to underestimate their significance. A victim who has not been
> physically harmed may find that his or her friends consider the
> crime a minor incident, no matter how the victim feels about
> it. They think they know what serious crime is—they've seen
> enough of it on television.

> Few victims are prepared for the aftermath of victimization, the ways that a crime can echo and reverberate against the rest of the victim's life. (Bard and Sangrey, 1986, p. 7)

When it comes to the needs of victims, historically professionals have not shown much more awareness than the media. Although being the victim of a violent crime can be a devastating personal catastrophe, prior to the mid-1970s the counseling and behavioral science literature rarely mentioned it.

Perhaps even more damaging than ignoring the victim is the tendency, even among professionals, to blame the victim. Abrahamsen (1973) postulates a theory that victims of violent acts are driven by unconscious motivations to arrange their own destruction.

> That the victim, through provocation and seduction, plays a large part in the execution of a violent crime, must be brought to the attention of the public. To avoid becoming a victim of murder, assault or rape will, in the last analysis, depend on how well the person is able to refrain from getting emotionally involved with someone who is potentially dangerous to one's life and welfare. . . . There is little doubt that many such victims could have avoided their fate had they been able from the beginning to scrutinize carefully their own motivations. (p. 42)

This tendency to ignore or blame the victim must affect the ways in which victims cope with and give meaning to their experiences.

THE VICTIM RESPONSE

Researchers who have studied the problem have noted that violent victimization seems to elicit observable patterns of responses (Bard & Sangrey, 1986; Everstine and Everstine, 1983; Figley and Sprenkle, 1978; Ochberg, 1977; Rahe and Genender, 1983; Symonds, 1980). They present various models that attempt to bring some order to the understanding of the psychological aftermath of victimization (see Figure 1). There exists, however, considerable variation among the models. Despite many unanswered questions about the after-effects of victimization, there is little doubt that victims are affected, usually injured, by their experience.

Figure 1
Post Trauma Recovery Stages

AUTHOR	MARTIN SYMONDS (1980)	CHARLES FIGLEY (1985)	MORTON BARD AND DAWN SANGREY (1986)	RAHE AND GENENDER (1983)
VICTIM POPULATION	VICTIMS OF STREET CRIME AND FAMILY ABUSE	DEVELOPED FOR COMBAT VETERANS APPLICABLE TO VARIED VICTIM POPULATIONS	ASSAULT VICTIMS	VICTIMS OF CAPTIVITY
STAGE/PHASE SEQUENCE	1. Shock, disbelief, denial phase. Paralysis of action.	1. Catastrophe phase. Continues until victim feels safe.	1. Impact-disorganization phase. Feelings of isolation, fear, self-doubt.	1. Brief euphoria (first seconds to minutes after release).
	2. Frozen fright, pseudo-calm, detached phase. Traumatic Psychological infantilism.	2. Relief and confusion. Relief event is over, confusion about why it occurred and eventual consequences.	2. Recoil phase. Denial, reintegrative efforts.	2. Hyperarousal (first minutes to hours). Returnees have difficulty handling the excessive stimulation right after release.
	3. "I am stupid" phase. Alternating phases of apathy, anger, depression, resentment, phobic reactions, constipated rage.	3. Avoidance. Temporary effort to blunt the pain with denial.	3. Reorganization phase. Painful experience is assimilated and put into perspective.	3. Compliance/resistance (first hours to days). Increasing resistance as feelings of power return.
	4. Integration into lifestyle phase. Development of defensive-alert patterns.	4. Reconsideration. Confrontation of trauma and its meaning.		4. Denial (first days to weeks). Denial of any ill effects due to their traumatic experience.
		5. Adjustment. Trauma is successfully incorporated. The victim becomes a survivor.		5. Restitution (first weeks to months). Needing to "make up for lost time." Readjustment problems common.
				6. Gradual readjustment (first months to years). Dealing with the long road to recovery.

Even where no physical harm is done to the body, the short- and long-term consequences may be profound. Victims may endure unexplained flashbacks of the event and are at risk for suffering chronic anxiety and depression. Their lives may be haunted by sleep disorders, stress-related medical problems, and marriage and family difficulties (Bard & Sangrey, 1986; Frederick, 1980; Kilpatrick, Resick & Veronen, 1981; Ochberg, 1978; Symonds, 1980; Terr, 1981).

HOSTAGE TAKING: SOMETHING UNIQUE

Although there needs to be considerable allowance for the way in which a victim phenomenologically experiences the degree of threat or violation, certain offenses seem particularly injurious to the survivor: rape, assault with bodily injury and a prolonged terror experience that often occurs with prisoners of war, kidnap victims or hostages. The often extended nature of a kidnapping or hostage experience introduces the variable of an ongoing interpersonal relationship with the perpetrator(s) during the course of a highly charged experience. It is not clear to what extent duration and relationships may serve to exacerbate, or even mitigate, the trauma of being held captive.

Jenkins (1976) in a Rand Corporation report, has described being kidnapped or taken hostage as

> one of the most harrowing experiences a person can be subjected to. No matter how short the period of captivity, it may be worse than the lengthy imprisonment of a convict. The sentence of the hostage is indefinite; it may end in release or death—the outcome is unknown, even whimsical, beyond control of the hostage. No prescribed set of rules can be followed to avoid punishment or execution. A hostage has no final hour to prepare for mentally as the condemned prisoner has. Nor, typically, is the hostage a member of an organized group as is the prisoner of war. Most often, he is alone. It is not simply a matter of being deprived of one's freedom for a few days; it is an agonizing game of mental Russian roulette. (p. 5)

Survivors of such an event offer a special challenge to counselors and psychologists to identify and meet their immediate and long-term needs for counseling. Some former hostages who sought professional help complained that psychiatrists and psychologists tended to look at them as "sick." A woman survivor of the Hanafi Muslim hostage-taking in Washington, D.C. said, "They think we have deep problems, and that's not the case. We have been bruised and battered, but we are not critically wounded. We just need a little help to get over a horrifying memory" (Fenyvesi, 1977, p. 115).

THE NEED FOR RESEARCH

A survey found that the directors of community mental health centers believe that "the form of services thought to be appropriate for victims was some form of counseling" (Kiresuk & Lund, 1981, p. 47). The same group, however, believed that "the amount of knowledge available about the needs of victims is not substantial" (p. 48). Many authors have echoed this observation and called for an intensification of victimization research (American Psychological Association, 1984; Chelimisky, 1980; Fattah, 1979; Frederick, 1981; Hartsough, 1988; Kiresuk & Lund, 1981; Ochberg & Soskis, 1982; President's Task Force on Victims of Crime, 1982; Siegel, 1983). The problems inherent in conducting such studies are formidable. Carefully controlled experiments that might approximate a trauma experience with human subjects are regarded as dangerous and unethical. Analogue studies with "safe" levels of stress may be useful but have serious problems in generalizing to real trauma experiences. Field studies, therefore, offer a valuable way to gather needed data on victims.

The research reported here is a field study intended to enhance our understanding of one population of victims: former hostages, specifically, correction officers who have been taken hostage during a prison riot. This qualitative study attempted to elicit the perceptions of these people and understand how they give meaning to the experience and their own lives years after the trauma has occurred. It is expected that a better understanding of the long-term implications of this victimization experience will enable counselors and other mental health professionals to improve the quality of their services to these victims. With adequate understanding, counselors can avoid interventions that are ineffective or offensive to the victims and offer counseling, support and other services that would meet the needs of this population.

To gain the understanding that has been called for, these interviews have raised, and tried to answer, questions along four dimensions. The first question is the most global: What meaning do hostage survivors, years after the event, give to their experience of being forcibly taken captive? What words, images, feelings and metaphors do the survivors use to describe the experience? As can be heard in their own words, the riots were experiences full of meaning and feeling for these men. Even in the unprepared speech of conversation, the power of the event for these men is vividly communicated in the words they use to describe it and their reactions to it. The source of that power is at least partially disclosed in the analysis of those words.

Because the nature and extent of the long-term impact of a hostage-taking has been unclear, the second area of inquiry explored this issue. The question asked was: what did the survivor view as the enduring negative or beneficial effects of the experience. It was the subjective perceptions of the hostage survivors that supplied the data used to answer this question. Their perceptions were quite varied. Some interesting generalizations, however, could be abstracted from the data.

Victims of natural disasters or violence often report strong feelings about their own behavior during a crisis. Feelings of pride, remorse, guilt, etc., it was observed, could have a continuing influence on the people involved. Therefore, the third question asked: How do hostage survivors view their own actions before, during and after the event? Relative to this issue, what effects has the hostage experience had on the way the survivors view themselves?

Another clue to the meaning of an event is the subjects' perception of other actors who are involved. In this study, the subjects' evaluations of the actions of others served to elucidate the meaning of the experience for the subjects themselves. Several questions were raised in this broad category: What are the perceptions and attitudes of hostage survivors toward the rioting inmates and toward inmates in general? What are the perceptions and attitudes of hostage survivors toward other persons in their environment, for example, administrators, fellow officers, family members, etc.? Do hostages report any changes in their attitude toward these people over time or as a result of the hostage-taking?

Several researchers have noted the similarities in the effects of various types of victimization (Bard & Sangrey, 1979; Frederick, 1980; Janoff-Bulman & Frieze, 1983; Lifton, 1983). It is useful, therefore, first to consider hostages in light of the theory and research on victims of other forms of traumatic stress, but especially person-to-person violence. One may be victimized by crime, natural disasters or social and political conditions. Subcategories may include rape, burglary, fire, flood, or being held as a hostage or prisoner of war. The intensity of the experience may be affected by duration, the nature and level of the threat and the nature of the material loss or physical suffering experienced by the victim.

Frederick (1980) contrasted the effects of natural and human-induced violence upon the victims. He found substantial similarities as well as some important differences. Reactions to both forms of stress often included "anxiety, insomnia, depression, anorexia, psychophysiological reactions and phobias about the event" (p. 72). Only victims of human-induced violence, however, tended to experience deep guilt about not preventing the event and about the plight of other victims. Moreover, they are more likely than victims of natural disasters to develop long-term cohesive feelings with other victims. Frederick goes on to note that "most victims were normally functioning persons prior to the event. They have been targets of severe stress and show signs of emotional and psychological strain as a result" (p. 75).

Other researchers also have found that even healthy, fully functioning persons are not spared the effects of a traumatic experience (Grinker & Spiegel, 1944; Merbaum & Hefez, 1976; Swank 1949; Ursano, 1981). Bard and Sangrey (1980) affirmed this observation: "any person who is subject to enough stress will be thrown into a state of crisis, and criminal violation of the self is more than enough stress for most people" (p. 29). Robert Lifton (1983) also maintained that, while one's vulnerability is relevant, it

> is only a matter of degree: if that threat of trauma is sufficiently great, it can produce a traumatic syndrome in everyone. . . .
> The survivor retains an indelible image, a tendency to cling to the death imprint—not because of release of narcissistic libido as Freud claimed, but because of continuing struggles to master and assimilate the threat (as Freud also observed), and around larger questions of personal meaning. (pp. 169–170)

In his concept of "the struggle with meaning" or "formulation," Lifton moves beyond the more easily observable "symptoms" and recognizes that trauma, even massive disasters, are ultimately experienced on a very personal level and have profound effects on the victim's "inner world."

Lifton (1967) saw, for example, that the "dropping of the atom bomb in Hiroshima annihilated a general sense of life's coherence as much as it did human bodies" (p. 525). Mastery of the experience, then, depends on re-establishing a meaningful structure that allows the survivor to confront the "death immersion," as well as his or her altered identity.

VICTIM RECOVERY AND SOCIAL SUPPORT

According to some authors (Bard & Sangrey, 1986; Everstine and Everstine, 1983; Wortman, 1983) the level and quality of social support is a major variable in determining how well one develops mastery over the victimization experience.

> If the victim's recovery is supported by other people, their help provides a kind of counter-balance to the violation, reassuring the victim of the essential trustworthiness of most people. The victim who receives appropriate help from family and friends, for example, will come out of the crisis with a heightened appreciation for them and a greater ability to seek their help again. Weathering a crisis can be a strengthening experience for victims and those who love them. (Bard & Sangrey, 1980, p. 24)

Pennebacker (1985) studied more than 2,000 people who had suffered trauma, including physical abuse, rape or bereavement. If survivors managed to confide in someone about the experience, they stayed healthier. Those who didn't talk about the event were more likely to suffer a range of health problems—from headaches to lung disease. Caplan (1974) concluded that when stress is high, people without psychological support suffer as much as ten times the incidence of physical and emotional illness experienced by others who have adequate support. Social support not only provides victims with the opportunity to talk about the event and vent emotions (Coates, Wortman & Abbey, 1979; Silver & Wortman, 1980), but also can help with practical problem-solving needs (Gottlieb, 1979; Hirsch, 1980).

Positive social support following victimization helps the victim re-establish a sense of psychological well-being, largely by enhancing self-esteem (Cobb, 1976; Kutash, 1978; Sales, Baum & Shore, 1984). Friedman, Bischoff, David, and Person (1982) found that the more supporters victims had, the sooner they recovered from the post-traumatic stress of victimization.

Other people in the victim's environment, however, are not always helpful. Others may tend to see victims as responsible for their fate (Frederick, 1980; Lerner, 1970; Ryan, 1971), thereby maintaining their beliefs in their own invulnerability (Janoff-Bulman, 1982; Lerner, 1980). Victims may be ignored because they are seen as losers (Bard & Sangrey, 1979) or because of a feeling of "contamination" or guilt by association (Frederick, 1980; Weis & Weis, 1975). Another reason for avoiding victims is that they are often depressed, and people usually prefer not to be around depressed people (Coates, Wortman & Abbey, 1979). Victims may at times, therefore, be socially isolated when social supports are especially important (Coates & Winston, 1983; Symonds, 1980).

A UNIQUE EXPERIENCE

While much can be learned by examining the effects of different forms of captivity, the hostage experience is, in many ways, unique. The future, for the hostage, is not as predictable as it is for the prison inmate— or even the prisoner of war. Concentration camp victims and prisoners of war are likely to experience a larger range of stressors—including starvation and torture—over a longer duration than hostages taken in the United States are generally forced to endure. POW's and prison inmates are usually young and male and have, albeit for very different reasons, agreed to engage in an activity that puts them at great risk. When they are captured, there can be some recognition that is is within the rules of the game. POW's, moreover, may view their suffering as meaningful and themselves as casualties in a worthwhile endeavor.

While certain groups, such as diplomats, psychiatric hospital staff, and correction officers, are at higher risk, hostage-taking often is experienced as having a random quality to it. The hostage often senses that he or she was simply in the wrong place at the wrong time. Eitinger (1982) noted that the hostage victim

> is a prize that is seized in order to be exchanged for something else. His importance lies only in the exchange value, so that he is considered essentially an object snatched randomly or by location or, occasionally, because of some connection with wealth, family, or business. Victims of hijackings or

hostage incidents are often simply regarded as symbols—
without personality or individual value. The question, "Why
me?" is often unanswerable. (p. 76)

The tendency to view the violence and stress of a hostage incident
as having no purpose could be an important determinant of the impact
that the experience has upon the survivors. Several authors have noted
that captives who have been able to identify some purpose to their lives
and their suffering were more likely to survive, both physically and
psychologically (Bettelheim, 1980; Frankl, 1969; Segal, Hunter & Segal,
1976).

In addition to the perceived randomness, unpredictability and mean-
inglessness of being taken hostage, there is, of course, the overt, often
overwhelming, threat to life that is present in a hostage incident. A
description of a 1980 prison riot in New Mexico conveys some sense
of just how severe the threat to life can be. On February 2, 1980, 17
correctional officers were taken hostage at a New Mexico prison near
Santa Fe. The 17 officers were held for 36 hours; six suffered from
multiple trauma, stabbings and fractures. The hostages described their
surroundings as "chaotic beyond belief." Electric power was interrupted
during the riot, and much of the penitentiary was in darkness. Dense smoke
filled the corridors; it was impossible to see anything but silhouettes,
making identification difficult or impossible. Six inches of water was
on the floor because of broken water pipes. Bodies of inmates who had
been beaten, killed, or had taken drug overdoses were scattered throughout
the institution. Although the prisoners controlled the institution itself, the
perimeter of the facility was surrounded by the state police and the
National Guard.

Many inmates had taken medication from the pharmacy, and they
were wobbly on their feet and talking incoherently. Armed and masked,
"execution squads" roamed the institution looking for victims. Other
inmates armed themselves with knives and clubs in self-defense. Many
of these inmates feared for their own lives and took overdoses of
medications so that, if they were to be killed, they would not suffer.
The sounds of destruction and the screams of inmates being tortured
and killed completed the picture of what one hostage said "seemed like
hell" (Hillman, 1981).

Hillman characterized the operative stressors in this incident as (1) a
feeling of total and profound helplessness, (2) existential fear stemming
from the certainty that they would be killed and (3) intense sensory input

that overwhelmed their mental processes. For months afterward all of the hostages suffered from sleep disturbances, involuntary re-experiencing of the event and anxiety. Interestingly, one hostage said that he felt "invisible," meaning friends, looking only at his outward appearance, could not understand how different he felt inside.

CHANGES IN ATTITUDE: THE STOCKHOLM SYNDROME

In a hostage situation, there are powerful social forces that can threaten one's self-image and even one's sense of identity. A hostage-taking is not a brief incident but a dynamic process with many variables operating in a highly charged atmosphere. The relationships among perpetrators, hostages and authorities are fluid. Dissension occurs not only between these groups but within them as well. Decisions by any faction may have life and death consequences, yet the decisions often must be made instantaneously based upon ambiguous data. For their part, hostages are forced into a submissive, powerless role and cut off from outside institutional and social support. It is not surprising that the experience, with all of its intensity and complexity, can effect changes in attitude and alliances with both immediate and long-term implications.

One response to being taken hostage, frequently discussed in journals and the media, has been termed the "Stockholm Syndrome." It is a response with real survival value for the hostages, but can complicate the siege management process and lead to troublesome social and psychological consequences for the hostage survivors.

The term "Stockholm Syndrome" was coined as a result of events that occurred on August 23, 1973, at the Sveriges Kreditbank in Stockholm, Sweden (Strentz, 1982). Jan-Eric Olsson punctuated the morning routine at the bank with bursts of submachine gun fire. Four of the 60 occupants of the bank were taken hostage in the bank vault and began a 131-hour ordeal that changed their lives.

The media gave extensive play to the behaviors of the hostages during and after the incident. The hostages gradually came to fear the police more than their captors. In a telephone call to the Swedish prime minister, one of the hostages expressed the feelings of the group when he said, "The robbers were protecting us from the police." Upon release other hostages puzzled over their own feelings and wondered, "Why don't we hate the robbers?" (Strentz, 1982, p. 150). Reportedly, one female hostage had sexual relations with the robber in the bank vault and continued to have affection for him well after the incident (Ochberg, 1978).

The Stockholm Syndrome has been observed in hostage situations with some frequency. The Patty Hearst story is probably the most famous. The phenomenon, it seems, is not universal, but it is fairly common. The situational and psychological factors that evoke the response have not been firmly established. Soskis and Ochberg (1982) have summarized the data that has been gathered:

> This syndrome, consisting of affection for the captor coupled with negative feelings toward the police, government, and sometimes the hostage's family, has been found in approximately one-half of recent terrorist hostage cases. Skilled interviewers of hostages feel that the incidence of this syndrome may in fact be considerably higher. The positive feelings toward the terrorist are often reciprocated, boding well for the ultimate outcome. The syndrome affects both sexes, all ages, and has occurred in all cultures observed. The manifestation of affection, as noted above, is determined by the age and sex of the dyad involved. Fatherly, fraternal, or romantic affection have all been described. . . . The intensity of feelings seems to increase during the days of captivity, stabilizes in the aftermath, and eventually diminish. (p. 123)

I observed this first hand when I debriefed an administrator and a teacher who had been briefly taken hostage in the hallway of their school by a disturbed parent with a shotgun. They were held at gunpoint for only twenty minutes, yet the seeds of the Stockholm Syndrome had already begun to grow. They reported feeling fear and anger at the police, whom they thought would burst in on the tense scene and create a deadly crossfire. The hostages did not want the burden of new factors to deal with added to a situation where they already felt helpless and out of control.

The perpetrator was arrested while trying to leave the school grounds and placed in a psychiatric facility for observation. The two freed hostages, for two days, expressed considerable concern for their former captor. They felt great compassion for him and wanted to be sure he was treated well. "He could have shot us and didn't," they often repeated. They unknowingly articulated a crucial element of the process that generates the Stockholm Syndrome. Instead of rage that they were unjustly threatened with violence, they were grateful that the violence was not unleashed.

By the third day, however, the two survivors became more aware of their anger. Instead of wanting to go check on the perpetrator's condition, they dryly joked about wanting to go to the hospital to hit him over the head. For other hostages, in different circumstances, the attitude change may be more durable.

Ochberg (1978) identifies four factors that seem to promote the Stockholm Syndrome: the intensity of the experience, the duration of the incident (although after three or four days, duration may be irrelevant), the dependence of the hostages on the captor for survival, and the psychological distance of the hostage from the authorities. Strentz (1982) observes that the Stockholm Syndrome develops through three phases. First, the hostage develops positive feelings for the captor. Second, the hostage develops negative feelings toward the police and other authorities. Finally, the captor develops positive feelings toward the hostages.

Most authors conclude that the Stockholm Syndrome is an automatic, unconscious response and not a rational decision to side with those who are calling the shots. Both hostages and hostage-takers are affected by the phenomenon, and it serves to unite them against the "outside threat." The psychological mechanisms that contribute to the radical attitude shifts that occur with the Stockholm Syndrome have been explained in various ways. Anna Freud's (1974) concept of "identification with the aggressor" is frequently mentioned as a psychodynamic explanation. This defense is generated by the ego to protect itself against threatening authority figures. The identification is born out of fear, rather than love. Its purpose is to avoid punishment or annihilation.

Ochberg (1978) rejected the psychodynamic explanations and proposed that the combination of denial and gratitude were the operative factors in the development of the Stockholm Syndrome. He suggested that hostages somehow deny the danger engineered by the perpetrators. Having separated this from their awareness, the hostages are overwhelmingly grateful to the captors for giving them life. The focus is on the captors' kindnesses and not their acts of violence.

AFTER THE TRAUMA

The various psychological models used to explain the attitude changes in hostage victims notwithstanding, there can be little doubt that the effects of a hostage experience are profound. Released hostages often feel embarrassed or stigmatized by the captivity experience (Wesselius & DeSarno, 1983). Behaviors that occurred during captivity as a result of the Stockholm Syndrome may contribute to feelings of shame, guilt and self-doubt. Moreover, several authors (Everstine & Everstine, 1983; Ochberg, 1982; Soskis & Ochberg, 1982; Wesselius & DeSarno, 1983) have noted problems with guilt in hostage survivors that seem to parallel guilt reactions in POWs and concentration camp victims (Bettelheim, 1980; Dor-Shav, 1978; Niederland, 1968; Segal, Hunter and Segal, 1976).

There may exist "survivor guilt" for having escaped the abuse or execution suffered by others. Additionally, a hostage may feel guilty about having been captured and think about things he or she could have done differently to have avoided capture or to have outwitted the captors. The survivor may be extremely self-critical as a result and may expect others to be critical as well.

This expected, and sometimes actual, criticism by others, as discussed earlier, can serve to prevent the victim from receiving the social support that may be necessary for recovery. Moreover, Symonds (1980) describes a "second injury" that occurs to victims who perceive a rejection by—and lack of support from—police, officials, family and society in general.

> This second injury often follows any unexpected helplessness.
> . . . After the initial shock and disbelief, the person becomes frightened, and his or her past feelings of security, safety and invulnerability are shattered. In addition, the person's idealized image of himself or herself as a self-sufficient, autonomous individual is damaged. These feelings of fright that occur even in the most resourceful individuals lead to clinging behavior. (p. 37)

This heightened sensitivity to the interpersonal distance of others may cause the victim to perceive others as uncaring or rejecting. Symonds suggested that victims feel twice betrayed by society: first for not protecting them from the terror and humiliation of the experience and second for failing to respond adequately to their victimization. As part of their rage, victims may avoid friends and family and become socially reclusive, even abrasive and unpleasant. Not infrequently, victims become phobic and develop hostile-dependent relationships with friends, family and sometimes with strangers. "They seem to act as if someone has to pay for their victimization and injured pride" (Symonds, 1980, p. 38). Symonds does not discuss how this other-directed rage co-exists with the self-blame described by other authors. Presumably, the raging at others could defend the victim against guilt, a potentially more threatening and painful emotion.

BENEFICIAL EFFECTS

An old proverb suggests that what is not burned by the fire is hardened by it. It is worth noting that not all hostage survivors regarded the experience as a totally negative event in their lives. For some, the opportunity to prove their courage or help others in tangible ways has made them stronger and shielded them from some of the harmful effects of captivity (Soskis and Ochberg, 1982). After a close brush with death, life may take on a deeper meaning. As steel is tempered by heat, a stark confrontation with mortality may provoke individuals to re-evaluate the past and seek deeper meaning in their lives and new directions for the future.

The story of one of the American diplomats, held hostage in Iran for 444 days, illustrates this phenomenon. During his stay he faced long and brutal interrogations, often throughout the night. He spent nearly 150 days in solitary confinement. His cell contained only a foul mattress and hordes of centipedes that marched across his face when he tried to sleep (Segal, 1986).

> No word from his family was allowed to reach him, and his existence was so cruelly regimented that he could urinate only with special permission. His relentless dysentery went untreated, and he shed a pound for every week of his captivity.
>
> In the stillness of one hot summer night, the hostage was blindfolded, stripped to his undershorts, and led outside for execution. He heard the cocking of the rifles ("I was praying the end would come quickly"), he remembers, but the triggers were never pulled. Small wonder that "every day thereafter, the presence of death was on my mind." (Segal, 1986, p. 102)

For months prior to his release, various "experts" offered their dire predictions of the effects of captivity on embassy personnel in Tehran.

There would be, it was pronounced, permanent emotional scars. The hostages would have lifelong problems in interpersonal functioning, neurological damage, and an overall inability to cope with the world. Indeed, some did suffer psychological injury from the experience. However, many of the Iranian hostages, like the man described above, rather than being devastated by the trauma, actually used it to enrich their lives (Segal, 1986).

> Like most of his comrades, the hostage emerged to freedom without lingering symptoms: no disabling anxiety or depression, no lacerating guilt, no insufferable problems readapting to the world he had left behind. Instead, he quickly regained his vigor, picked up the threads of his family life, and resumed his diplomatic career. Today, more than five years later, he is a leader in his community, and his mental health continues to be excellent. (Segal, 1986, p. 2)

Returned prisoners of war also have been examined in this regard. Of 221 released prisoners who responded to a questionnaire, 61 percent indicated that significant favorable mental changes had resulted from captivity experience. Only 32 percent of a comparable group of non-prisoner veterans reported favorable changes. The group who felt they benefitted said they were "more optimistic, believed they had more insight into self, and felt better able to differentiate the important from the trivial. Interpersonally, they felt that they got along better with others and claimed greater patience, human understanding, and appreciation of communication with others" (Sledge, Boydstun & Rahe, 1980, p. 443). Belz, Parker, Sank, Shaffer, Shapiro and Shriber (1977) and Segal, Hunter and Segal (1976) also found that a captivity experience sometimes brought families closer together and led survivors to rethink their philosophies and develop a greater sense of their own worth.

SYMPTOM CLUSTERS

Although stories of courage and human endurance are heartening, most observations of the actual hostage recovery experience are more sobering. A summary of the available data suggests that survivors of a hostage experience are at markedly greater risk than non-victims to experience a range of negative psychological effects. These effects may be broken down into six clusters.

Anxiety Reactions

Anxious feelings may begin shortly after the incident and continue or be triggered by anniversaries or other events. Certain people or objects may elicit a phobic response because of their perceived similarity to someone or something involved in the traumatic experience. Nightmares, nightsweats, hyperstartling, flashbacks, inability to concentrate and other symptoms of anxiety are common (Frederick, 1980; Hauben, 1983; Ochberg, 1977; Terr, 1981).

For some victims there is an inordinate fear of a second occurrence or a reprisal by former captors. The illusion of invulnerability is shattered, and the world becomes a terrifying place to be (Segal, Hunter & Segal, 1976).

Psychophysiological Complaints

Because a hostage-taking often involves physical, as well as psychological, trauma, thorough medical examinations are necessary. POW studies suggest that headaches, ulcers, heart disease and hypertension would be possible effects of a hostage experience (Segal, Hunter, & Segal, 1976). Victims of the Hanafi Muslim hostage-taking in Washington reported problems with diarrhea and sleeplessness (Belz et al., 1977; Hauben, 1983; Hillman, 1981). Problems with constipation, impotence and obesity also have been observed (Ochberg & Soskis, 1982; Rahe & Genender, 1983).

Siegel (1984) reported that some hostages experienced visual hallucinations. He found that the combination of visual deprivation, isolation, physical abuse, restraint on physical involvement and threat of death could produce hallucinations in 25 percent of victims. These symptoms ended when the hostages were freed.

Rahe et al. (1990) examined the returning hostages from the American Embassy in Iran. Their psychological testing was essentially normal. However, plasma and saliva cortical, urinary catecholaminies, and saliva testosterone were highly elevated. The physiological indicators reflected the ordeal that they had endured and probably the stress and elation of freedom.

Depression, Helplessness

Feelings of depression may occur after a hostage experience and may deepen as the victim's celebrity status, and any positive feelings associated with the dramatic event, fades (Frederick, 1980; Hauben, 1983).

The traumatic experience of powerlessness and helplessness may leave victims with persistent doubts regarding their personal efficacy. Painfully aware of this vulnerability and mortality, victims confront the unpleasant realization that they are never totally in control of their lives (Hillman, 1981; Symonds, 1980).

Guilt, Self-Doubt

Guilt and obsessive self-doubt regarding the victim's "failure" to prevent, or behavior during, the incident may occur. "Survivor guilt" may occur if others are perceived to have suffered more than, or instead of, the victim (Bard and Sangrey, 1979; Bettelheim, 1980; Everstine & Everstine, 1983; Niederland, 1968; Segal, Hunter and Segal, 1976; Simon and Blum, 1987; Ochberg & Soskis, 1982; Wesselius and DeSarno, 1983).

Anger

Because perpetrators are unavailable, victims may generalize their anger onto others. Alternatively, victims may be angry at clinicians, officials, friends or family for their failure to prevent or adequately respond to the victim's trauma (Frederick, 1980; Simon and Blum, 1987; Symonds, 1980).

Impairment of Social Functioning

All of the above problems, especially anger, anxiety, guilt and depression can lead to significant problems in marital relationships, child rearing, occupational activities and friendships.

In writing about victim responses, many authors note similar effects. Several have offered persuasive arguments that identifiable patterns of victim recovery do exist (Rahe & Genender, 1983; Symonds, 1980). These same authors, however, have noted considerable variation in the severity and duration of victim-related effects. Explanations for such variability are tentative and often look to existing psychological theory, not to victims themselves, for their foundation. It is not clear how specific characteristics of the victim and his or her perceptions of the perpetrator and the event may interact to influence the nature and duration of effects upon the victim. Moreover, a number of authors have hypothesized that the victim response is not a static phenomenon but evolves over time (Bard & Sangrey, 1979; Figley & Sprenkle, 1978; Rahe & Genender, 1983; Symonds, 1980). They have proposed varying models of victim adaptation, suggesting that victim after-effects, as well as coping mechanisms and support needs, may change over time. This further complicates an already challenging area of services for helping professionals.

THE LONG TERM

The President's Task Force on Victims of Crime (1982) has stated that "the mental health community should study the immediate and long-term psychological effects of criminal victimization" (p. 105). Clearly, there is a need for research on almost every aspect of victimization, but perhaps least is known about the long-term consequences. Shortly after a trauma, people are more likely to be supportive and attentive to the victim. Victims are more likely to feel that they are able to seek support and counseling without being stigmatized. Employers and family may be tolerant of behavior that otherwise would be unacceptable. After a period of time, however, perhaps several weeks to a year, there will be an expectation that the victims will put the experiences behind them and "get back to normal." If victims are still dealing with the effects of the trauma, they may unconsciously deny or deliberately conceal the problems, again with unknown long-term consequences.

Hauben (1983) noted in a follow-up of Dutch hostages that 68 percent reported "long-term" after-effects of a hostage experience. These after-effects were consistent with trauma reaction: anxiety, phobias, psychosomatic complaints, disturbed sleep, nightmares, irritability, disturbed concentration, lability, and depression. Victims also reported feeling misunderstood, insecure, threatened and preoccupied with the hostage experience. A few hostages reported positive effects such as improved self-esteem and greater attention from others. Hauben observed that the positive effects did not appear to persist over time. It is very important to note that the definition of "long term" used in this study was "after four weeks."

Hauben tried to relate characteristics of the events and of the hostages to the severity of the after-effects. He found that certain factors could be used to predict negative after-effects: a more negative experience, younger age of the hostage, less education, greater degree of affiliation and pairing off during the incident, poor physical health prior to captivity, longer duration of captivity and the psychological rigidity of the victim.

It is impressive that Hauben was able to interview 168 people, 59 percent of the Dutch hostage survivor population of 283. Another 15 people returned surveys. Of the respondents, 88 percent believed that their problems had not previously existed. The other 12 percent thought their complaints were exacerbations of previous problems. The victims overwhelmingly regarded their experience as very harmful.

Van der Ploeg and Kleijn (1989) further examined the survivors of the series of eight large-scale hostage incidents that occurred in the Netherlands in the 1970s. Of the nearly 500 ex-hostages, a third were found to suffer from negative after-effects of their trauma. Symptoms generally echoed the DMSIII-R diagnostic criteria for post-traumatic stress disorder and generalized anxiety disorder. Survivors also suffered from a variety of medical symptoms. Of the former hostages, 12 percent were found to be still in need of professional after-care.

The available data is sufficient to state with some confidence that hostage victims are affected by their experience, usually negatively, perhaps for quite a long time. What is not well-known is how they make sense of it all on a very personal level. We do not know what meaning they give to the experience and how that meaning–giving process is related to the way in which the hostage survivors integrate their experiences into their daily lives. Such is the focus of this book.

2

The Search for Meaning

What really got to me was, it was the first time—let's say in fifteen years, I think somewhere in that area—that the inmates frightened me. They got to me. The first time in fifteen years working for the department. That had never happened. And that bothered the hell out of me. (John)

This comment by a hostage survivor points to both the nature and the value of the research method used in this study. Fundamentally, this study was an attempt to uncover the meaning that informants attributed to the events in their lives. By understanding meanings and perceptions, not merely actions, we can begin to explain behavior of individuals and their view of themselves and their world.

For the man quoted above, it was not the fear alone that affected him, stemming though it was from the threats, the beatings and his view of a noose awaiting his neck. What really "bothered the hell" out of him, more than the fear itself, was the fact that they had *made him afraid*. They had won. He had lost—lost control and power. Perhaps most critically he had lost his view of himself as a fearless man in the midst of some of the most violent men in the nation. Other hostages focused on their concern for their family, trying to escape, fear of pain or endless other possibilities, each giving very personal meaning to his experience of a very public event.

This study was about the diversity, and the similarities, of perceptions of men who have been intimate with terror. It was an attempt to find out what they can teach us about the long-term adjustment to being taken hostage, an experience where one is held captive, under constant threat, in a highly charged atmosphere with an unpredictable outcome. It is very much a "real world" experience that is not easy to replicate in a laboratory or other controlled setting. Even if possible, it is doubtful whether such an experiment would be desirable or ethical.

Moreover, many investigators have become increasingly disillusioned with the laboratory paradigm as a vehicle for providing useful information about how people react to highly stressful events (Bulman & Wortman, 1977; Lazarus & Lannier, 1978; Wortman et al., 1980). It has been observed that there are fundamental differences between stressors encountered in a laboratory and those experienced in the "real world."

Many laboratory studies have exposed subjects to a number of repeated stressors such as shocks or noise bursts. Outside of the laboratory, however, people rarely experience a string of identical stressors delivered within a short time span. Further, laboratory stressors may not elicit from subjects a significant investment in the purpose or outcome of the study. Experimenters usually provide a "cover story" to explain why subjects are being exposed to the stressor. Subjects are given the opportunity to leave the experiment if they do not wish to participate. On the other hand, undesirable events in the "real world" often happen without foreknowledge and for no known purpose or reason. Moreover, some of the most significant reactions to undesirable events, such as changes in self-concept, may develop slowly over time and are not amenable to study in short-term laboratory research (Wortman, 1983).

Studies involving deception generally are considered unethical and may be permissible only if the experimental variables will not cause suffering and if the variables may be counteracted, should they be aversive (American Psychological Association, 1982). Even without deception, however, studies that approximate real life stress may be too risky. Zimbardo's famous (1975) prison simulation study using fully informed college students had to be terminated early because the "inmates" experienced such severe psychological and physical stress reactions.

It becomes clear, then, that field research can be an important component of an effort to understand the experience of violent victimization. While laboratory studies suggest that changes in cognitive and affective processing may be a consequence of experiencing stress (Monat &

Lazarus, 1977), relatively little is known about the nature and subjective meaning of these changes. Discerning how people think about events, how they formulate assumptions and expectations they have about themselves and their world—this is the focus of qualitative research. How hostage victims perceived their victimization and themselves, how they gave meaning to their experience—these phenomena were the focus of this study.

This qualitative approach assumed that the victims' perceptions were, as Bard and Sangrey (1986) concluded, "central and valid" in understanding their victimization. Post-victimization data on the frequency and severity of various psychiatric and medical symptoms does not communicate what it is like to be a hostage victim. Statistical data leaves invisible the internal processes that may be linked to the more easily observable symptoms. Qualitative data derives from the actors themselves—generating hypotheses, not testing them.

MEANING AND PHENOMENOLOGY

Phenomenology, essentially, is the study of how things appear to people *prior to* their various theories and constructs. The counseling profession has deep roots in the phenomenological tradition—often associated with Carl Rogers (1961). This qualitative study, in its conscious attempt to uncover and understand the victim's perception and assumptions, was consistent with that tradition. The design of the study, however, was not chosen so much to be traditional as to acknowledge the value of individual perceptions and assumptions in the study of victims.

From day to day, people operate on the basis of assumptions and personal theories that allow them to establish goals, plan activities and order their lives. This set of assumptions has been variously labeled our "assumptive world" (Parkes, 1971, 1975), "theory of reality" (Epstein, 1973, 1980) or "structure of meaning" (Morris, 1975). Being a victim of violence challenges the assumptions individuals have about themselves and their world and may impair their ability to function. As Bard & Sangrey (1986) wrote, victims experience a "loss of equilibrium. The world is suddenly out of whack. Things no longer work the way they used to" (p. 14). Lifton (1976) noted that whether one is a victim of rape, a combat veteran, or involved in a natural disaster, the survivor may feel acutely aware of a change in personal identity.

Even some behaviorally oriented investigators have noted the importance of meaning in stress–response situations (Haward, 1960). Lazarus, Averill and Opton (1974) give the concept of "appraisal" a primary role in their interactional model of coping. They maintain that whether a situation is threatening or gratifying to a person depends on how it is interpreted, and such an interpretation is derived from the cognitive structures that a person has acquired over his or her lifetime.

The importance of meaning in understanding traumatic events did not escape earlier writers. Following his experiences in Auschwitz, Victor Frankl (1969) posited the need for meaning as a fundamental human motivation. Freud (1926) stated that "physical stress and psychic trauma cannot be equated because psychic trauma is not so much determined by the physical intensity of a situation as by the meaning and affects evoked in a particular individual." Lidz (1946) pointed to the need to understand the meaning of an event to an individual rather than just accepting the event as a trauma too great to be withstood.

With this phenomenological orientation, the qualitative method can provide access to this meaning—giving process. This can allow one to understand better how hostage victims view the events that are imposed upon them and how these individuals struggle to rebuild their assumptive world after they have been victimized.

SYMBOLIC INTERACTION

This study's efforts to uncover and reconstruct individual reality through in-depth interviews is a phenomenological research method that is guided by the theoretical framework of symbolic interaction. This approach has roots in the work of George Herbert Mead (1934), Herbert Blumer (1969) and W. I. Thomas (1931). According to Blumer, symbolic interaction rests upon three assumptions:

1. A person acts toward a thing based on the meaning the thing has for him.
2. The meaning of a thing is derived from the social interaction one has with others.
3. Meaning is managed and modified by an interpretive process used by the person in dealing with the things he encounters.

Accordingly, Blumer (1969) does not regard meaning as "emanating from the intrinsic make-up of the thing" (p. 5). Meaning constitutes the "real world" within which individuals live their lives. As Thomas (1928) noted: "It is not important whether or not the interpretation is correct—if men define situations as real, they are real in their consequences" (p. 572).

Glaser and Strauss (1967) developed a grounded-theory approach that enhanced the ability of investigators to apply symbolic interaction constructs to real world research problems. They posited that qualitative research should not be merely a rich description of people and things but should be conducted in a way that moves the data toward high levels of abstraction.

One way to conduct qualitative research involves carefully preparing oneself with a review of the relevant literature before doing rather narrowly focused work in the field. This approach can lend itself to the study of very specific phenomena when one has very specific questions. An alternate strategy involves trying to avoid potentially limiting preconceptions by not reviewing the literature in advance. One is advised to immerse oneself in the field, making observations and taking notes that are as literal as possible. Interpretation and theories are, at this stage, to be avoided.

The grounded-theory approach of Glaser and Strauss rejects these two extremes. Acknowledging that preconceptions exist anyway, they advise using them as "sensitizing concepts" that can help one begin the process of asking questions and gathering data. The sensitizing concepts are not firm research orientations. They are readily abandoned as one gathers data that helps to confirm, deny or transcend initial preconceptions. The experimental scientist's narrower focus of proving or disproving a stated hypothesis is avoided. Moreover, there is an attempt to establish cause–effect relationships.

The qualitative researcher assumes that a person's definition of a situation is a part of the meaning of the situation. It is necessary, therefore, for such research to stay close to the source—the participants themselves. Given this orientation, qualitative researchers may utilize a range of strategies to gather data generated by subjects: review of documents, participant observation, case studies and in-depth interviews. The unpredictable and episodic nature of a hostage-taking event, and this study's retrospective character, pointed to the appropriateness of the in-depth interview for data gathering.

LIMITATIONS OF THE STUDY

In considering the study's limitations, several issues should be noted.

Researcher's bias is an issue in all research methodologies; qualitative research is no exception. Unstructured interview formats may be particularly vulnerable to interviewer bias. The interviewer may transmit prejudices through subtle cues. This bias, while never eliminated, was minimized through maintaining a certain self-consciousness about the process. Following the recommendations of Bogdan and Biklen (1982), field notes were written to encourage and record self-reflective process observations. The affective experience of the researcher, emerging themes and ideas, assumptions and expectations were all documented in an attempt to acknowledge and manage researcher bias. These efforts proved very helpful. Moreover, the sheer volume and weight of the data itself tended to squeeze out the false assumptions and prejudicial attitudes. One example involved the researcher's expectation that middle-aged correction officers would have great difficulty accessing and verbalizing their affective experience. This proved untrue as the men generally spoke eloquently and movingly about their emotions and experiences.

To some degree, a known observer generates and obscures data in ways that cannot be fully known. The very presence of a person asking questions creates an environment and a dynamic that is different than it would have been. As with research bias, one can only minimize, never dismiss observer effects. Bogdan and Biklen (1982) advised qualitative researchers to "interact with their subjects in a natural, unobtrusive, and non-threatening manner" (p. 43). Thus, subjects usually were seen in a private, comfortable room in their own home. Two were interviewed in motel rooms and two in their offices. There were no readily observable differences in the nature or quality of the data relative to location. Wherever interviewed, the researcher strived to establish a trusting, positive rapport. The names of mutually known and trusted third parties were mentioned, and strong assurances of confidentiality were given. The researcher's connection to corrections and the general purpose of the study was shared. Subjects were encouraged to verbalize any questions or reservations. An attempt was made to respond satisfactorily to any concerns.

Another limitation of the study concerns the subject population. Subjects were exclusively middle-class males who grew up and resided in various parts of upstate New York. Except for one black man, they were all white. Except for one man in his late 20's, they ranged in age from late 40's to early 60's. They all worked in, or retired from, the New York State Department of Correctional Services. While their similarity of background and shared experiences fit the framework of this qualitative study, the subjects were in no way a random or representative sample of some larger population. It is readily acknowledged that other populations of hostages may be different in significant ways. Qualitative research, however, approaches the issues of generalizability differently than quantitative research. As noted by Bogdan and Biklen (1982), qualitative researchers assume "that human behavior is not random or idiosyncratic. They therefore concern themselves not with the question of whether their findings are generalizable, but rather with the question of to which other settings and subjects they are generalizable" (p. 41).

This study purposefully reached for the distant view. Little was known about what survivors think of their experiences and themselves years after a hostage-taking event. Subjects for this study reflected on hostage experiences that occurred in 1970, 1971 and 1983.

Subjects were taken hostage at three different times and places. This variable was welcomed. The study did not look for perceptions of, and reactions to, a specific historical event as much as a personal response to the essential experience of being taken hostage in a prison setting. For example, Biklen (1973), in a retrospective study of women's perceptions of the elementary school experiences, used subjects who had gone to different schools and had backgrounds that differed along many demographic variables. With qualitative techniques for data gathering and analysis, such differences can enrich a study.

Correction officers, being a high-risk group, offered a population with at least limited availability for study. Moreover, factors relating to role reversal, prior relationships and institutional settings raised intriguing questions and offered a logical focus for analysis. Early informal contact and discussions with hostage survivors in corrections indicated that survivors had vivid memories of the experiences and were usually eager to talk about them. Therefore, 12 current and retired correction officers, who experienced a hostage-taking, participated in the research. Before approaching the last few interviews, there was a large volume of data. Categories to be used in analysis could be readily differentiated. The volume of data permitted these categories to become "saturated."

Subjects were identified through an informal network of correction officers. Potential subjects were often suspicious or reticent at first. Mentioning the names of two or three known and trusted members of the Department was usually necessary to obtain an interview. All participants were male and ranged in age from 28 to 62. Four of the men had retired from corrections work; eight were active members of the Department. Their marital status varied; one was never married (the youngest), one was single by divorce, ten were married. It was a second marriage for only one man.

Interviews were conducted at places convenient for the subjects. Settings were arranged to be quiet, private and as comfortable as possible. Interviewees were initially suspicious of the purpose of the tape recorder. However, they consistently relaxed after they were given assurances of confidentiality, the purpose of the study was clarified and they were given control over stopping or erasing the tape whenever they wished. No subjects exercised their freedom to edit the audio tape on the spot. In fact, after the initial reluctance, some seemed pleased and flattered that a researcher felt their stories were important. My being identified with certain trusted officers and officials within the Department did much to build credibility and rapport with the men interviewed. It seemed unlikely that the subjects would have agreed to participate in the study, or have been so open in the interviews, if I had not been so strongly recommended.

Despite such recommendations, eight hostage survivors who were contacted by telephone declined to be interviewed. Three of these were relatively younger men who had been involved in the Sing-Sing riot. Two of these said they would participate only if the study had approval from the Central Office in Albany. Such approval had earlier been denied. Other refusals came from men who indicated that they felt uncomfortable talking about the riots—specifically Attica and Auburn. One Attica survivor spoke directly of the issue in a terse reply on the telephone: "No, it's been sixteen years and I still have nightmares! I don't want to talk about it. I'm sorry." The reply itself raised questions about the group who did agree to talk with me. I wondered if those who did agree to talk were less harmed by their experience or had somehow more effectively dealt with it. While there was no attempt to utilize random sampling, it is important to be aware that the subjects in this study may have differed from the men how refused to participate or those who had long ago left corrections.

INTERVIEWS

Data was acquired by use of what Borg and Gall (1983) termed "un-structured interviews." Also termed "non-directive interviews" (Meltzer & Petras, 1970), with this approach the researcher attempted to establish rapport with subjects, introduce certain issues and then give the subjects freedom to explore their perceptions, feelings, memories and beliefs. Subjects were encouraged to introduce topics relevant to them and their experience. A particularly rich line of discussion could be followed as long as it seemed fruitful. Follow-up questions were asked to clarify an issue or enhance understanding. Bodgan and Biklen (1982) advised the use of open-ended questions to elicit more expansive replies. This strategy was followed during the interviews.

Subjects were invited to reflect on their perceptions of the hostage-taking incident itself, their view of themselves before and after the event, their beliefs about the short- and long-term consequences, people, things or ways of coping that helped them get through it all and what meaning it all had to them years after the event. Respondents were encouraged to answer from their own perspective and with their own words.

Borg and Gall (1983) believed that such "unstructured" interviews were particularly appropriate in situations where the type of information sought is difficult for the subject to express or is potentially distressing to the individual. This observation accurately reflected the researcher's experience. The researcher was able to use interview skills to allow for variation and spontaneity within the interview process while still directing the dialogue toward the focus of the research.

There were 12 interviews ranging in length from one hour and 15 minutes to three and one-half hours, making a total of slightly over 31 hours of transcribed interviews. Comments made by subjects after the tape recorder was turned off, and other observations by the researcher, were noted and written in the field notes for each interview.

Bogdan and Taylor (1975) recommended several guidelines for conducting interviews that were included in the study's procedures:

1. Allocating enough time for each interview.
2. Tape recording interviews in an unobtrusive manner.
3. Developing rapport and trust with the subjects before probing more sensitive areas or challenging his or her statements.
4. Creating a receptive, open atmosphere during the interview by refraining from interruption, by assuming a non-judgmental stance and by paying very close attention.

Events and perceptions reported by respondents may not have corresponded precisely to an objective, historical account of events. The passage of time, the desire to present oneself in a positive light, or distortion caused by the traumatic incident itself may have affected how respondents reported data to the interviewer. However, whether or not events and behaviors were consistently reported as they actually occurred is not crucial to the study. The task of the study was to examine the perceptions and beliefs of hostage survivors—not their actual experiences.

Nevertheless, it was not necessary to accept interview data totally without scrutiny. The interviewer was able to observe a range of obvious and subtle non-verbal behaviors. For example, if a subject cried or if his voice faltered, face reddened and jaw tightened, one could conclude with some confidence that the material evoked a genuine response on an affective level. His actual verbal report of events, however, may not have been "objectively" accurate or even subjectively truthful. Further, if a person reported information that reflected on himself in an unfavorable or embarrassing way, as some did, it was likely that the data was accurate, at least in the view of the respondent.

Subjects seemed to accept assurances of confidentiality and had no obvious external demands on them to distort the truth. A number of subjects witnessed and reported the same events without any variations that were suggestive of deliberate distortion. Minor differences in their verbal reports seemed more readily attributable to differences in physical location during the events and individual differences in the way they subjectively perceived or remembered the action.

In the study of a victim readjustment following assault, Sales, Baum and Shore (1984) noted that their study shared a problem endemic to all those obtaining victims at some point after the victimization experience: the need to rely on retrospective data on the incident and adjustment. In their study, victims varied widely in the time between assault and the research interview. The researchers checked the effects of these differences and found the victims to be "remarkably similar in their reporting of pre-assault and immediate post-assault symptoms. No differences due to memory fading were found" (pp. 118–119). They concluded that the traumatic nature of the victimization experiences may have etched them more deeply into the memories of victims. All participants were informed of their rights as research subjects and interviewed in accordance with American Psychological Association guidelines.

DATA ANALYSIS

Data from interviews and field notes received consideration as it was gathered in order to enhance the collection process. Staying "in touch" with the data pointed to particularly productive directions and clarified issues in the research. Most of the formal analysis, however, occurred after the data was collected. At that point it was sorted and coded into 41 categories.

Coding Categories

1. Administration	22. Going Back
2. Fellow Hostages	23. Anxiety
3. Family	24. Denial
4. Hostage Takers	25. Unmet Needs
5. Other Inmates	26. Other Officers
6. Sexual Assault—Fear of	27. Anger
7. Threats	28. New Attitudes
8. Physical Abuse	29. Why Me?
9. Acceptance of Death	30. Role Reversal
10. When It's Over	31. Being in a Group
11. Communications	32. Effects
12. Fear of Unknown	33. Memories
13. First Sign of Trouble	34. Retaliation
14. Escape	35. Other Hostages
15. Perception of Self	36. Humor
16. Helplessness	37. Control
17. Time	38. Sexual Problems
18. Media	39. Aggressiveness
19. Negotiations	40. Depression
20. Survivor Guilt	41. Support
21. Alcohol/Drugs	

Some codes became apparent during the field research. Other codes were generated as the data received closer scrutiny.

It is believed that the characteristics of the subjects, the current state of our knowledge about the long-term effects of victimization and the ability of qualitative methods to reach beyond what is known, or even hypothesized, made this design appropriate to this research problem.

3

Captivity and Chaos: The Riots

Prison riots and violent hostage-takings are events that, fortunately, most people have never experienced. In order to provide some context for the discussions to follow and to convey some sense of the nature of these events, the uprisings are described below. The information is drawn from newspaper accounts, official reports and, primarily, the descriptions of hostage survivors.

AUBURN

It started on the morning of November 4, 1970. There was a mood of anger and protest in the nation, and this mood had penetrated the walls of Auburn Correctional Facility. Two days earlier, on November 2, a group of nine black Muslims had forcibly taken control of a loudspeaker platform and made some incendiary speeches. The incident ended without violence, and the inmates were assured by one officer that they would not be punished. This policy was reversed at a higher level, however, and the inmates were ordered into keeplock—confined to their cells for a certain number of days. This enraged many inmates, especially blacks, and the tension level in the facility mounted. Before breakfast on November 4, the inmates were making speeches and confronting correction officers about the "broken promises" and the "unfair" punishment of the nine Muslims.

All the inmates finished breakfast, and about 600 of them gathered in the main yard. Many of them surrounded a sergeant in the yard and angrily confronted him.

> Well, they finally let him go. He was to go up to the front to inform the administration on what the inmate demands were. And then this big crowd dispersed to some extent. There were little pocket groups all around and then of course there was, as usual, an awful lot of noise in the yard at that time . . . and then everything grew deathly still. Not a sound in the yard and that is when you know something is coming. It gets real quiet . . . real, real quiet. And then you can look out the yard; there is not one inmate standing in the middle of the yard. But they were lined up all around the yard with their backs to the walls of the blocks. All around me. And then [pause] slowly, but slowly, you would see one inmate go into one block, come out, another inmate go into a block, come out, another inmate go into a block, come out. They were going in for weapons, going to pick up shanks and so on and so forth. (John)

Groups of 35 to 40 inmates, armed with homemade weapons and tools from a prison construction site, approached officers in the yard and in the cell blocks (housing areas), relieved them of their nightsticks and took them captive—about 40 guards in all. They received various threats; some were repeatedly beaten. They were held in a tight circle in the middle of the yard. The hostages were closely guarded to prevent escape and to keep the more reckless or psychotic inmates from having their way. The hostages were given blankets to ward off the cool November air. The blankets were doused with gasoline to ward off would-be rescuers.

Outside the walls, the City of Auburn mobilized for a disaster. Officials feared that the inmates would attempt to break out of the facility, which was located in the heart of a residential neighborhood. Schools were closed early, and the students, some of them children of on-duty correction officers, went home and told their mothers rumors about prison breaks and officers who were stabbed and killed.

Inside the prison, hundreds of police officers, state troopers and sheriff deputies massed—and waited. Negotiations continued. By midafternoon, the inmates decided to surrender. The hostages were all released, two at a time. The riot was over.

ATTICA

About a year before the Auburn riot in 1970 there had been an uprising at a New York City correctional facility often called "the Tombs." Many inmates actively involved in that event worked their way through the correctional system and were eventually assigned to Auburn. Auburn was perceived to be a highly secure facility and could, it was believed, handle difficult inmates. Many of the leaders of the Auburn riot, and other troublesome inmates from around the state, were sent to Attica. Some inmates, therefore, had repeated experience with taking control of a correctional facility. For maximum control, many of these inmates were concentrated at Attica into one "company" of 50 men.

As at Auburn, experienced officers at Attica were aware of a growing tension within the facility. The special company in "A" block was particularly disruptive.

> They had even punched a lieutenant in the chest, which was totally unheard of back in those days. This particular morning [of the riot, Sept. 9, 1971] they feared that they were going to have more problems with them, so they locked the yard and wouldn't let them out in the yard. When they reached the yard door, a lieutenant named C—— went down to explain to them that he wasn't going to allow them to go into the yard. They had to return to their cells. As soon as he got there, they started hitting on him and the officer that was escorting him. And that was it. It took off from there.
>
> They ran back to centergate. They jumped on this gate. Well, apparently way back when that prison was constructed, the contractor . . . there was a rod that went up into the ceiling and into the floor. And they were a little short of materials and they welded about four inches on the top of one of those rods. The weld broke. The door opened and they took over the prison. That's how the riot happened at Attica. (Richard)

Forty-eight hostages were initially taken in the uprising. Two more were hunted and captured after the media announced the names of those who were among the missing. One officer died from blows to the head suffered when the riots began. Ten hostages died from gunshot wounds suffered during the assault. Thirty-two inmates died. Many other inmates and correctional staff were injured.

The four and one-half days, Sept. 9–13, 1971, became etched into the memories of officers, troopers, family members and the nation. There were intense feelings of fear, helplessness and apprehension. Family members agonized. Some local shopkeepers ran into the streets with shotguns, having heard a rumor that busloads of inmate-sympathizers were on their way to take over the town. Heavily armed assault personnel stood by, tense and apprehensive, wondering what it would be like to storm the trenches and fortifications that were being constructed on the other side of the wall.

The hostages were kept in a circle in the prison yard. They choked on the acrid smoke from numerous fires. They wore inmate clothing and were often blindfolded. They watched, or heard, the debates among the various inmate factions. Some wanted a few hostages executed to "show they meant business." Some psychotic inmates contributed to the general chaos, going around attacking inmates and hostages alike.

All this was endured for four and a half days. Then the siege was over, and a massive and violent assault finally ended the uprising. It was the bloodiest encounter between Americans in this century.

SING-SING

The tension started mounting when the second shift came on duty at 3:00 PM on January 8, 1983.

> There was a new sergeant. He was new to me but I guess he had been there for awhile. He decided that anybody that wasn't in their cells at this particular time was supposed to be locked up which is something that almost never happens in Sing-Sing. But he gave us all orders to go around and find anybody that wasn't in. We had to lock them all up and that is just totally against what normally is done at Sing-Sing. They didn't lock up anybody for anything down there, you know. But this day we got there and for no reason we got to lock everybody up. You

do that and that gets everybody, you know, everybody is a little pissed about that.

From there it was . . . it ran pretty much normal from then on until after chow, which is about five o'clock. Six o'clock we were supposed to let everybody out . . . they would let them out, you see there are 800 people in this block. Not 800, about 650 maybe. But he decided that nobody was going anywhere. Okay? Then he lets out a company, maybe 80 inmates, and he runs them down and just stops. Stops for no apparent reason. That lasted for almost an hour and now everybody is really getting upset. I don't like this guy. He had been drinking. So after this hour is up and everybody is nice and agitated, then he decided to let everybody out. Somebody jokingly asked, "Are we going to let out the keeplock too?" He decided that was a good idea! Those are the people, those are the ones we had to lock up. You're not supposed to let them out for anything—well, something major like a fire or something. Letting keeplock out, you just don't do that. But he decided to let them out. Thirty or forty inmates wanted to know what the deal was. He told them all to "get fucked." It was his block and they will do what he wanted them to do. During this time, you know, it was really loud. You get 600 people yelling that, the whole world can hear them. (Jerry)

The inmates' rage mounted until it was time to lock them up for the night. They had to be locked in by ten o'clock, but the process took a long time. Built in 1825, the fortress-like structure had outdated locking systems. Officers were sent into the blocks. It was like throwing a rock at a hornets' nest.

The inmates got all riled. It was pretty much of a quick thing. It wasn't really planned . . . at least not by the inmates. That was it. They started tearing the place apart. They were grouping everybody up and C—— [the sergeant who had been drinking] on the way out took the keys and he got out. That's how it was. (Jerry)

Eighteen officers were taken in this ordeal that lasted three days. Hostages were made to wear prison greens and were subjected to a barrage of threats and occasional beatings. Inmates blocked entrances with barricades and intricate boobytraps. Inmates walked around wearing sheets and hoods, carrying knives and spears and other weapons. Hostages were kept in cells alone or in pairs and were frequently moved. After three days the uprising reached a negotiated end. It was considered a success for the State's relatively new Crisis Intervention Team.

A WORLD APART

These descriptions, and others to follow, unfold stories of fearful events that occurred in an alien world. In conducting the interviews and touring prison facilities, the researcher at times felt like an anthropologist studying an exotic culture. Indeed, prison institutions exist as a kind of society complete with its own language, currency, industry, laws, courts, customs and hierarchy. Mostly, the community at large is content to ignore the routine processes of life occurring within the borders of this peculiar society.

The riots, however, galvanized the attention of those on both sides of the walls. These anomalous events opened a window onto a scene that was already strange. The hostage-takers, in a real sense still captives themselves, found themselves on a very large stage indeed. Attica, in particular, commanded worldwide attention.

In the midst of this astonishing and confusing maze of reversed roles, suspended rules, multiple actors, uncertain leadership and alarming events, the hostages maintained their singular focus on survival. Later they would rail against the perceived negligence or malfeasance on the part of prison administration. The preponderance of information regarding the riots would incline a reasonable person to find some justification for the anger of the hostage victims. Justified or not, as the hours or days passed without a negotiated end or a rescue, the hostages felt a mix of anger, helplessness and fear. The anger toward those in authority was, among the hostages, general, strong and persistent.

The three riots described above were events that would clearly fit the American Psychiatric Association's (1987) criteria for a traumatic stressor: an identifiable event that is of such a magnitude that it would be expected to "be markedly distressing to almost anyone, and is usually experienced with intense fear, terror, and helplessness" (p. 247). The hostages also experienced some of the same stressors experienced by concentration camp survivors: (1) protracted life-endangering situation, (2) prolonged helplessness, (3) recurrent terrifying episodes and, (4) assaults on self-esteem and self-image.

Being held hostage by inmates in a maximum security facility is undeniably a traumatic experience. It is, however, an event so removed from normal experience that it is difficult to comprehend. The descriptions above and the accounts to follow, it is hoped, will make the human reaction to these events more comprehensible.

THE SIEGE: IMPRISONED BY PRISONERS

"How does it feel to be on the other side, man?" (Auburn inmate) The thirty-four-year-old correction officer, hands tied, a length of pipe held over his head, didn't respond. Twelve years in the department had not prepared him for this moment. The truth was, it felt awful.

The hostages in this study experienced many things during their hours or days of captivity. To understand the meaning of these experiences years later, it is important to consider how these men perceived the events and themselves during the crisis itself.

FIRST REACTIONS

The men interviewed consistently spoke of a growing uneasiness prior to the uprisings. "The inmates started milling around; just felt different in there. So we knew something was going on" (Steve). Sometimes the danger signs were more overt. Several officers were sent down to reinforce a worsening situation in the prison yard.

> Well, in doing so, in this little walk we were taking, we passed some of the officials of the prison making their way out of the yard in a hurry. One was the captain and one was the sergeant. And I said to the captain coming up, "What's going on?" He said, "Things don't look good." And he didn't even stop walking. He just kept right on going. And the sergeant, he was just "vroom" [gesturing]. He was just motoring right

out of the yard. He wasn't even going to talk or nothing. He was *gone*!

So we kept going and I could see the inmates. They were all lined up against the walls and the middle of the yard was empty, which, you know, when you see things like that happening, you know something is not right. (Bill)

Poor communications in the facilities, and perhaps their own disbelief, made it difficult to ascertain the seriousness of the situation.

I didn't know anything about it. I just had come back from those two days off. I really didn't know what was going on. Communications were slow in coming . . . the communication within the prison itself, the telephones, there was no radio. There was no security, P.A.—personal alarm system. There was nothing. (Steve)

Being new, I didn't know what was going on. (David)

The worst of it was, just not knowing what was happening. We tried to keep order. It was not that much disruption. It was just that everybody had milled around. That's when the uh . . . fear of the unknown came in. What is going to happen? (Joe)

The shock and disbelief immobilized victims, preventing them from taking action in time. One informant in the study observed an officer clearly being escorted by an inmate, but it did not register that the man was a captive. Other employees discussed among themselves what should be done about securing gates and keys, delaying action until it was too late. One experienced correction officer, who had been relieved of his stick and stripped of his clothes reported,

No one really thought about escape or trying to . . . trying to get out the back, which we probably could have. But you also, you always had that feeling of security . . . and not knowing exactly what was going on. Of course, I think people were

a little different back then. Maybe it was the way we were
brought up. I don't know. (Steve)

Another officer, having seen clear indications that a revolt was starting,
remained oblivious:

It didn't bother me. No. We more or less had to push our
way through to get through, we were going down to the main
blocks and almost like being nice saying, "excuse us" so we
could get through! You know [laughter] and I mean there was
a riot going on, you know! (Erik)

For some hostages, this denial, their failure to comprehend fully the
meaning of events, persisted for the duration of the six-hour Auburn
riot. After enduring hours of chaos and threats, seeing other hostages
beaten, one twelve-year veteran of the Department remained relatively
calm. When asked what was going through his mind during those hours
in the hostage circle he responded, "Well, not as much as should have
been. . . . It really didn't dawn on me how serious it could have been
until I got out of there" (Philip).

TAKING COMFORT IN THE GROUP

The survivors of these prison uprisings frequently mentioned the re-
assurance they took in being placed with other hostages. As one man put
it, "I had, you know, a lot of guys there with me and if I was with only
three or four, I would have felt a lot different about it" (Philip). A hostage
from Sing-Sing put it more strongly: "I was really scared they would split
us all up, you know? Put different ones here and there and lock us up all
over the place. But they didn't. They kept us together" (Jerry).

This officer was later placed by himself for a night, and his anxiety level
increased dramatically. "The next morning," he relates, "I got into another
cell with another officer. It felt good to be with someone else" (Jerry).

There was a general sense that if you were with others, things couldn't
get too bad. Hostages sometimes would be taken off alone—usually to
get their assistance in breaking into some secured area. The captives
experienced this with great apprehension, fearing that they were being

led away for execution. The apprehensions sometimes carried with it some bitterness. "After a while, some of the inmates came for me and took me out of the circle of hostages. Nobody tried to stop them. Nobody protested. Nobody asked where I was going—or anything else" (Ron).

Another example shows how meaningful it is when a man does receive that much-craved support. It occurred shortly before the Auburn incident ended, and the man was visibly moved as he shared the story.

> It went on like that for the afternoon and, I would say, early evening, when things started breaking a little bit. I know that when I was taken out of the yard—I was one of the last ones to be taken out I remember—I do remember a lieutenant being in that circle with us. And that lieutenant they were going to take out of the yard and he refused to go. This was a heck of a nice guy. You don't find too many like him. He was . . . he refused to go until all his men were out of the yard. . . . He was here on [temporary] assignment from Elmira at the time and he refused to go out of the yard until all the officers were out of the yard. (Erik)

A SPECIAL CASE

A hostage-taking in a correctional institution is a unique situation. A reversal of roles occurs that gives the event a special dynamic—the victims may say, a special horror. The implications of this are not lost on the inmates or the hostages. The officers would hear things like, "How's it feel? How's it feel to be on the other side? How's it feel knowing you aren't going home to see your wife anymore?" (Steve).

Many of those interviewed normally took pride in staying in tight control of their assigned areas, sometimes with odds of several hundred to one. One survivor noted wryly, "I don't like being told what to do by somebody other than my wife or my superiors" (Brian). When the inmates took power, however, their control over the hostages was perceived as absolute.

> And when I got there, the lieutenant was standing out there and I said, "Lieutenant, what are we going to do?" He says, "You do what they tell you to do." So, you know even with a lot of guys I knew out there with me, we were scared shitless,

> because these guys meant business. There was no ifs, ands or
> buts. If you didn't move, they were either going to put you
> down or they were going to move you, either one. And you
> know, when you start to put up, you know, a struggle, I knew
> it was useless. There was no sense in trying to do anything
> about it. (Bill)

These men were used to being unafraid in situations that would make most people very frightened indeed. Being frightened of inmates had a special meaning for these officers. One of them said, "They put the fear of God in me. I was just . . . it bothered me that the inmates really got to me" (John). This same man tried to go back to work after two months and lasted only a week. His anxiety was too intense. It was a second blow to his self-esteem and his view of himself.

> I just told the sergeant that I couldn't cut it. I got to go up
> front. I got to get out of here. And he got another officer. I
> went up front and talked to the Deputy Superintendent for a
> minute, B——, and uh, and that got to me. When they were
> able to get to me again. That got to me too. . . . It bothered
> me a great deal. (John)

The man blamed his subsequent, almost deadly, problem with alcohol and drug abuse on the fact that they had "got to him." They had penetrated his defense and shattered his image of himself and his way of coping on the job. No longer could he see himself as strong, brave and in control.

It is interesting to note that the language these men used to describe their job conveyed a sense of strength, competence and control. This can be seen clearly in the words of an Auburn hostage.

> **B:** If I had been in my kitchen basement (his usual post), I am
> firmly believed I would never have been taken hostage because
> there I control my destiny.
>
> **C:** You controlled that area.
>
> **B:** We had gone through a set-to on Monday afternoon where they
> were going to take over the yard and everything else. I had
> done certain things down in that area to protect the inmates
> and myself. Certain things I was going to do. (Brian)

The language that the same man used to describe his capture conveys a very different tone. Often he uses the passive voice.

> At a certain point in time, the action came on me. . . . Now, of course, I was up in this strange and hostile place. I was posted at a block that I was not familiar with when I was taken hostage at approximately 10:30. I was grabbed at approximately 10:30 and then the "hostage circle" was born probably half hour to forty-five minutes later. And I was herded with approximately 50 of us altogether by the time noon rolled around. (Brian)

The word "herded" provokes images of passive sheep or cattle being moved about at someone's direction. It articulated their humiliation and seemed to come up often in the interviews.

> In a little while we were all *herded* back over to the center of the yard. (David)

> And as they get us all together, all the officers, and they put us in the middle of the yard. And when they got to the middle of the yard, they *herded* us about like cattle, you might say, into the middle of the yard. (Bill)

One man used the word four times in the space of four sentences.

> So the rest of the population was being *herded*. They actually *herded* people. The kitchen crews were *herded* up out in the corner. If they weren't part of that, they were *herded* off in certain places to be used for the certain few who were trying to get their points across. (Brian)

It is difficult for individuals outside of the institutional culture to fathom the depths of humiliation experienced by the hostages in these riots. Loss of control and humiliation, however, were not their only problems.

BEATINGS AND THREATS

Even before the deadly police assault on the prison yard on September 13, 1971, Attica was a very violent uprising. Thirty-one correction employees were injured during the first hours of the inmate takeover. The Attica Commission Report (1972) contained descriptions of the injuries sustained on the first day, for example:

Raymond Bogart: Blows to head resulting in severe bleeding and loss of consciousness.

Robert Curtiss: Blows to face and back with pipes and sticks.

Don Jennings: Blows to head and back resulting in severe head bleeding.

Willie Quinn: Severe blows to head (resulting in death on 9/11/71).

Arthur Smith: Blows to head, kicked, became unconscious. (pp. 503–505)

One officer, who bravely tried to protect the keys stored in his office, gives a more personal perspective than the Commission's matter-of-fact report.

R: Captain L—— told me "the inmates are in your block." I didn't have any idea what he was talking about and I turned around and looked and there is a guy with a football helmet and a ball bat in his hands standing right in my door. Well, I pushed him out into the hall and slammed the door shut and then they of course jumped on the door and tried to pull it open and I was holding the door. And ah, there was a little window in the top of the door; they broke that out. And they were trying to reach me and uh, hit me with sticks and stuff. They couldn't reach me. I was crouched down holding the door closed. Well, oh, J—— [another officer] was trying to get some wire and things to secure it. And they poured some chemicals in on me and tried to set me on fire. They . . . I don't know what it was. They would throw burning rags in as they would do that, J—— would stamp those out. Then they went around behind us and they were spearing me in the upper back with mop handles—the points of the mop handles—trying to get me to release the door.

We took this off and on for er . . . a half hour or forty-five minutes. Uh. Finally, someone apparently had come through and had tried to get the door open. Must have been very strong. Broke the handle off the outside of the door so they couldn't get any grip on it . . . So then someone, I believe up in "Times Square" they got a hold of some gas equipment and they threw a large gas grenade into that very small room.

C: Right into your office?

R: Yeah. We had an extreme concentration of tear gas in there and I was concerned about that after it was all over that I had lung damage. But fortunately, I didn't and I never had any bad effects from it . . . And then they brought in the acetylene torch from the shop and cut the door open and they took us.

They took everybody else out but me and they didn't take me because they had told me on several occasions that they were going to kill me if I didn't give them the keys out of my vault in there. And I didn't do that, and uh, so when they got the door open they took the others out and told me I had to stay. And three of them stepped up in front of me and said, "We said we told you and now you are going to get it." Well there wasn't much I could do anyway because I had been banged up pretty bad up to that point anyways. My fingers were swollen on my one hand. I couldn't even use that. And I had extensive damage to my upper back. (Richard)

This officer's likely execution was averted through the intervention of another inmate, who, through pleading and intimidation was able to prevent further violence.

Another officer reported:

J: Went down with a fight. Got my ass kicked. Although they didn't get the keys they were looking for. No, they didn't get the keys they were looking for.

C: How badly were you injured at that time?

J: I just got a working over with the fist. I got, you know, I got popped a few times. It wasn't by everybody, you know, just a nailing. (John)

He was left alone for a while and then:

J: They came and got me again and they wanted some more keys and they took me back to the jail office. They frisked me; demanded the keys for this, for that, or something else. I didn't have them. I got worked over again. You got worked over for general principles now . . .

C: Yeah.

J: And they kicked the shit out of me. And that is basically what that was. It was freebees then. See? (John)

Another Auburn officer recalled in remarkable detail his experience.

One of them had a handle from a stretcher and he was jabbing with it. The guy next to me got hit right below the eye, right on the edge of the eye, and it split open here [gesturing] and he went reeling back. And they the guy next to him, who had come down from the second floor, he got hit right square in the eye, umm . . . and he lost his vision in the eye. And at the same time . . . I got hit two or three times in the hand and . . . uh . . . there was no future in holding onto the door like that because every time you're getting your hand battered like that. (Ron)

Although some hostages were not severely abused, many did report being "punched." They usually reported this in a very casual way, as if to downplay the significance of the blows. This relatively "minor" violence, however, may deserve further consideration.

During the course of gathering data, this researcher toured four maximum security facilities and one medium security facility. Making one's way past the razor wire fences, concrete walls, electronic doors, steel gates, guard towers and cameras leaves a lasting impression on the uninitiated. My apprehension at such times grew when, upon entering inmate housing areas with only one or two officers, I discovered that I was mingling with hundreds of prisoners who were coming and going with, apparently, little restriction. I remembered that these men were imprisoned, almost exclusively, for crimes of violence.

The correction officers, seemingly few in number, ran the normal gamut in appearance, tall and short, thin and overweight, etc. The inmates, on the other hand, leave a different impression. They appear unusually muscular and physically well-developed. Physical activities and bodybuilding are popular pastimes in a prison and are pursued vigorously for leisure as well as self-protection. There is ample time to pursue these interests, and it shows. Being punched by one of these men who was in an angry mood, in a highly charged atmosphere, could hardly be a casual event. A tall, muscular inmate, turned loose with a length of pipe or a baseball bat, would be a formidable antagonist indeed.

The threat, the fear of what could happen, seemed to have more of an impact on many hostages than the actual abuse they withstood. The words and actions of the hostage-takers made it difficult to overlook the dangers that were present. The hostages spoke of how threatened they felt.

> It was not knowing what they were going to do next. Some of the officers were taken off and beaten pretty good . . . others were not hardly touched. I got a few coming through B Block . . . most of it was uncertainty. (Steve)

> If you didn't agree, their justice was very swift. At least they proved it to me in '71. (Joe)

> And they had . . . behind each officer, they had maybe 30, I guess, 33 or 34 officers, behind each one they had an inmate with gasoline and a knife or a hammer or anything, you know, and they took the truck and aimed it right at the hostages. We see the truck coming and we think—they're going to run us over. . . . There were just threats all day. (Philip)

It was just as frightening at Sing-Sing.

> The little guy I told you about, P——, went first and he got clobbered with a two-by-four by this guy. He was doing nothing and he got clobbered anyway. And it was during the move and they gave me a washcloth to try to fix him up a little bit the best I could . . . it wasn't much. . . . I was expecting to get the shit kicked out of me. (Jerry)

Three different Auburn hostages shared the same frightening recollection—a fellow officer being struck on the head with his own stick. All gave a slight shiver as they related the incident. "Jesus, I see uh, him hit the officer in the head about three times with a club. Knocked him on the ground. Well, then I knew, you know, Bingo!—it was going to go" (John).

For two of the informants, the sound of the attack seemed to affect them more than what they saw.

> I know D——. I saw D—— get hit with a stick. I will never forget that sound, you know . . . it was a stick [subject winces]. (Ted)

This friend of mine who worked in C Block, evidently he wasn't going to give his stick up. And the inmate that was trying to get it from him cracked him over the head with it and "Boy!"—you could hear it ring through the yard, and he went down on the ground with it . . . oh, it was bad. (Bill)

One may be able to begin to imagine the scene, described similarly in all three incidents: the threats, the chaotic movement, the hostile faces, the angry shouting and intense noise, the pain from wounds and bound hands. Power and control among the inmates slipped back and forth among those who would protect the hostages and those who would kill them. One description of the Attica yard moves beyond intense and, at times, takes on a quality that is almost surreal.

S: So when it finally came down, um . . . the Black Panthers wanted to kill us Sunday afternoon.

C: The Muslims were protecting you, the Panthers wanted to kill you?

S: Yeah. The Panthers said that was enough. "We'd show 'em" whatever it was and they, well, they were ransacking part of the prison, they took, they ransacked the Chapel and they had all the robes and fancy clothing, I should say . . . they were all dressed up [voice cracks, long pause]. That's all right. But uh . . . the Panthers wanted to kill us to show the administration because they were very, very mad. . . . There was one of the inmates that was feeding us, giving us water, whispered in my ear that . . . he said, "I'm sorry, but I can't help you." And he says, "Nothing I can do." And he went away. (Steve)

CONFRONTING DEATH

All of the hostage survivors interviewed were physically abused or believed that they would be. Many feared that they would be killed. For some, it went even deeper than that. They fully believed that they would be killed.

Yeah, they played head games. "I feel like killing somebody today—and if I kill anybody, I'm going to get you first, you skinny runt," and things like that. I was . . . damn it, it was nerve-wracking. It was a day that I wouldn't want to wish on anybody, because you don't know if you're going to get out of there. And I didn't think we was going to, at the time. (Bill)

The speaker in the following quote moves from past tense to present tense. One wonders if it is the power of the memory that makes it more immediate.

There was one point there where I wondered if this is the end, am I going to die this way? [They said] the hostages will be wasted. I remember somebody somewheres that had gotten a fire axe. God knows where the hell they got a hold of one of those things. And I remember they laid their fire axe on my shoulder and I was scared of dying because I didn't want to die with a fire axe. I could . . . shoot me or something, you know? But I don't, I don't want my head chopped off with a fire axe. (David)

When a human being actually confronts death—not merely danger—but his impending, violent death, some fascinating things occur. One feels humbled at the prospect of trying to understand the personal meaning in such a profound and intricate experience. The interview data, however, opens a window onto an unusual and important phenomenon.

When the interviews turned to this topic, the men would speak more hesitantly, their voice would often crack and their eyes would fill up. One man, thinking death was imminent, said his thoughts turned to his wife. Another said he "was thinking about the kids. It was a long day. I didn't think I would ever see them again" (Bill). He then quickly changed the subject to what they were fed for lunch. Another man was slightly more indirect in alluding to his concern for his family: "I wished I had more insurance" (Ron).

While thoughts of loved ones dominated, some hostages experienced a certain fatalism that even seemed helpful in the situation. "I've always been a believer that when your time comes, it comes whether you're, you know, walking down the street or whether you're . . . whatever" (Ted). Accepting, what the hostages believed to be, the inevitability of their own deaths granted them a certain equanimity, even peace.

S: I figured it was coming, one way or another, because everything was dusted. From the way the inmates were talking, it wasn't,

> you know, it . . . I don't know whether we accepted it or what
> but I figured I was dead.

C: Yes.

S: What the hell. This was it. Either they are going to cut my throat
or someone is going to shoot me.

C: Felt resigned to that.

S: Well, what are you going to do? But before that you were helpless. I mean knees knocking—the whole works. I didn't piss my
pants or anything like that crap either, but . . .

C: Until you decided you were going to die, then things were
calm.

S: Nice and calm. Piss on it. What are you going to do? (Steve)

Once they accepted death, they could approach the next task more
calmly: how to die. In the midst of chaos and captivity they managed
to grasp that they still had some control, if only over themselves. Once
dying seemed a certainty, the only thing left was to decide *how* they
would die.

> I did a lot recollecting that day because I really didn't know if
> we were going to get out of there or not . . . I think we were all
> wondering the same thing, whether or not we would hold up to
> all this, because we didn't want to show any weakness. (Bill)

A survivor of Attica recalled, with a great deal of emotion, what he
thought to be his final decision.

R: There was only one thing that, you know, that was on my mind.
There was not any question that I was going to die. I mean I
accepted that. You don't want to die. You do everything that
you can possibly think of to prevent it . . . but you reach a point
where you *know* it is going to happen.

C: When did you believe that was going to happen?

R: I think probably sometime during the siege and I realized that
no one was coming because they hadn't arrived there yet.

C: Trying to hold out.

R: Trying to hold out. And the only thing that, to me, I could think
of was that I had two sons. Now I know I am going to die, I

know it is too late to go out and buy a lot of life insurance and take care of all that. And uh, the only thing I can leave them is *how* I die . . . That's it.

C: That's everything . . .

R: That's it. You don't want to grovel. You don't want to be on your knees. That's all.

C: To maintain your dignity was your goal at that point.

R: That's it, you know, that's all. That's all I thought of. It was very important.

C: Yes.

R: That . . . I say it to myself, you know, "Die like a man" . . . even now . . . [gets emotional]. It's heavy. Tough thing to think about. That's what it was. What it all condensed right down to. There was nothing else. (Richard)

Surviving a face-to-face encounter with one's own annihilation leaves one with certain scars—and creates special opportunities. The long-term meaning of all this will be examined later.

HOSTAGES AND THE STATE

The most consistent finding that came out of these interviews was the feeling the hostages reported while they were held captive. To a man, they felt anger—even rage—at someone or some group in authority. Far more anger was expressed at prison or state officials than at the inmates. There was some foregone acknowledgement that the inmates were mostly violent, untrustworthy people. It was assumed that they would try to take over if given an opportunity. The inmates, according to this same unspoken reasoning, did what they were *supposed* to do. The administration, however did *not* do what it was *supposed* to do: prevent a riot from occurring. There were frequent complaints that senior officers in all three facilities were too lax, maintained poor discipline, used inadequate procedures, etc.

The administration knew that something was going to happen there within a very short period of time . . . and I don't think they did anything to, you know, try to offset the thing before it got started. (David)

> The administration had been warned and warned and warned
> and things were getting bad. (John)

If the hostages were angry at the administration's incompetence, they were even more upset at the perceived lack of support coming from the authorities. This was true even for the hostage who had been involved in the more recent Sing-Sing uprising. As a new recruit, he had some hostage-survival training and knew the specially trained and equipped CERT (Corrections Emergency Response Team) would be on the scene. It seemed to make little difference. There were still feelings of anger and abandonment. "You were a hostage and they [the State] weren't going to listen to you. . . . They gave the impression that they didn't really care about you, and that's the State" (Jerry).

As the first minutes in captivity became hours, or hours stretched to days, and no rescue came, resentment deepened.

> I was thinking about where was the Goddamn help! You
> know—where was the State Police? What is going on? This
> type of thing. What's happening? You know. How come they
> are not in here? (John)

> I was wondering what they were doing out there and why we
> were still there. Yeah. Why are we still in this predicament?
> (Joe)

> There was a big feeling of let down. . . . People didn't do,
> didn't get you out quick enough. They didn't, nobody was
> doing anything. Everybody was hesitant. Then when you find
> out afterwards that you were partially right, you know, that
> don't help either . . . I think, some of the hostages did have
> anger like "Why do you do all this shit [waiting] and then you
> end up doing it [mounting an assault] anyway. Why did you
> leave us go that long? I have kids. . . . " (Steve)

Another Attica survivor put it succinctly: "You're angry at everybody, because no one came to your assistance" (Richard).

Two of the men interviewed hinted at, and then reluctantly explained a belief that was a source of an even deeper rage and mistrust. One officer was in the Auburn riot in 1970, and the other was in the 1983 Sing-Sing incident. Both went beyond accusations of administration incompetence and made allegations of conspiracy against the Department of Correctional Services.

> **P:** The lifers were more or less running it and they were doing . . . these other groups were doing all the work. [Pause] I always thought that some of them were put in there to cause this. 'Cause they were, you know, just to disrupt the system. I always felt that, I don't know why. It was probably wrong, but I always had that idea.
>
> **C:** Some of them were put in there . . . ?
>
> **P:** . . . purposely, to disrupt the prison . . . I always had that idea. (Philip)

The other man went even further with his suspicions. He noted various signs and "incidences" that added up to something very meaningful for him.

> **J:** I could tell that it really wasn't the inmates that did this . . . it seems to me that it wasn't planned [by inmates] because if it was planned they would have had the whole jail. 'Cause Sing-Sing isn't set up for security.
>
> **C:** Mhmm . . .
>
> **J:** It seems like it is, but it isn't . . . I think the State set them up to do this. I don't know. I guess maybe it was a good thing they did because if the inmates decided to do it, then I guess things would have come out differently.
>
> **C:** You think that the State set them up?
>
> **J:** There were too many coincidences. There were three women scheduled to work that day in A block. They actually showed up to work and they told them to go home. And there were some male officers that the inmates just cannot stand—and wanted them dead. And they weren't there either . . . Oh, and the other thing. We'd moved, the day before this happened, two days before this happened, we moved in three, four fags. They got the shit raped out of them.
>
> **C:** Got badly raped . . .
>
> **J:** Better them than me . . . I don't know just how high up the ladder this thing got, but I have my ideas. . . . (Jerry)

These men were very vague about the possible purposes of such conspiracies; nevertheless, they had very strong suspicions. It is difficult to say with certainty what led to their beliefs. Several explanations come to mind: paranoia, an extreme result of anger and suspicion toward authority, the need to believe that some force—even a malevolent one—was in control, or, even, a correct assessment of the facts.

In any event, it is clear that the hostages' isolation from authority, fear of injury and impatience with rescuers made a fertile ground for the growth of mistrust and anger at officials. Taken with the presence of some helpful, even "compassionate" hostage-takers, the emergence of the Stockholm Syndrome would be a logical development.

The large numbers of people involved and the sharp role and identity differences between hostages and inmates may have impaired the more complete development of the syndrome. Strong identification and even affection between hostages and captors was not observed.

When the event was over, all these beliefs and feelings did not simply go away. The hostages carried with them painful memories and, for better or for worse, a changed view of themselves. They faced the accusations, praise or apathy of those around them. When these men walked through the gate to freedom, the challenge they faced didn't end—it merely changed.

WHEN IT'S OVER

One can partially discern the personal meaning of an event by observing what happens when it is over. The baseball player who kicks the dirt after striking out, the moviegoer who gives a tension relieving sigh at the end of a horror film, the client who vigorously shakes the counselor's hand at the end of the session—all are communicating something about the way in which they experienced the event.

Two of the hostage-takings ended by negotiation. The Attica uprising was quelled by the infamous and bloody assault. Although the hostages were remarkably similar in their perceptions of events during their captivity, there was somewhat more divergence in how they subjectively experienced things when the incidents came to a close. The variation did not appear to be related to the location of their captivity. Moreover, there was still much that they seemed to share in their experiences and perceptions after the event.

For all the hostages, there was no "winding down" to a foreseen ending. They were generally in the dark regarding negotiations or events beyond their holding area. A number reported that when they were led to freedom, they did not know whether they were to be released or executed. Some told of the agony of being on the verge of freedom and then seeing their hopes dashed.

J: It was four distinct times that we were getting ready to get out and something would happen.

C: Collapse.

J: [Nodding] Negotiations came down, one time they even got real close. They had so much as pretty much cleaned it up and getting ready to get out and this . . . some asshole, some Senate Commissioner of corrections or something . . . he gets on TV and he says, "The hell with them. No amnesty." They didn't like it at all. (Jerry)

I know that when I was taken up I got as far as the sergeant's booth where the sergeant has his area in the yard and they [the inmates] said that they just heard on the radio that they had taken female hostages, you know. They told them to take me back to the yard. That was the toughest part; that hit me. Right there. (Erik)

After finally being released, one Auburn officer turned around and went right back to work. He normally supervised the kitchen, and he felt he was needed there to get the feeding program going again. He continued working twelve hour days for two weeks straight. Later in the interview, this same officer spoke at length about the importance of one's commitment to his job and to being a professional. He had, perhaps, chosen to do what was most adaptive for him at that moment: reasserting his control and authority in familiar surroundings.

For most hostages, their release was a climactic moment, characterized by powerful emotions and physiological reactions. One officer who had said he was aware of only mild concern during his captivity was overwhelmed when he walked into freedom.

When I went through the main yard door . . . coming into the main yard is when it hit me. That's when it hit me. Didn't hit me until I was, and I was home free, then I . . . I . . . just fell apart. You know, I guess I probably broke down and cried and really, I don't know. Just, I remember falling apart at that time. You know, I just, just all of a sudden hit me. Up until then it didn't bother me. (David)

The man continues, almost perseverates, beyond this quote talking about his intense experience upon release. It seemed as if his denial that helped him cope during the crisis, caved in when he was finally safe. This experience of feeling overwhelmed was echoed by others.

I can still remember that feeling that ah . . . when they let us through the lower hall, that's the administration building, that door closed behind me and I knew I was safe. Jesus! I can just . . . my knees, I can still feel them buckling, you know? (Joe)

I got up front and went into an office and I tell you the truth, I just broke down. Everything came out. It really did. All alone. There was no one with me . . . I went in and closed the door and I just, you know. Thanked my lucky stars. . . . So I went downstairs and I went to a pay phone. I must have been crazy because I could have gone to any phone. But I went to the damn pay phone to call my wife. I thought I am not going to the hospital, I will be okay. I just wanted to go into the pay phone and—man I went out. Just keeled right over. Passed out. (John)

After leaving the prison grounds, a few hostages went directly home. Most sought to be with other hostages or correction officers involved with the riot. At Sing-Sing, they took advantage of the opportunity to stay together at the hospital for a few days. Hostages from Auburn and Attica gathered at the VFW or local bar. There they talked for hours and consumed large amounts of alcohol. They were "wired" from the experience and sought ways to calm down.

I recall we went up to the VFW a short time after that. We had a few drinks [said with a knowing smile]. I am not a whiskey drinker or anything—I have a few beers—that's it. I remember that night, though. I got into the booze. But I was into the booze pretty good, you know, I bet you for a couple of weeks. (Ted)

There was a lot of talking among fellow hostages. A feeling quickly developed that no one else could understand what they went through. So they talked to each other frequently for weeks—sometimes through the night.

> We went all over it. We didn't know who got out, who didn't. So we found out afterwards. Uh . . . some of the guys got wounded. Some of the guys were killed. Some of the inmates got wounded. Some of them got killed. Of course, at the time I wasn't really worried about the inmates so much. (Steve)

The anger that the men had built up while they were being held grew, rather than dissipated, upon attaining freedom. Some felt that the administration did not care for them or the ordeal that they had just gone through for the Department.

J: You know, I could say very honestly, nobody really cared. They really didn't know, so they really didn't care. They say we were cry-babies. I had to go back to work the next day. When it happened a year later at Attica, they said, "Well, take six months off and let us know when you're ready to come back."

C: Yeah.

J: When it happened at Sing-Sing, they took them right to a hospital to be checked by a psychologist and a psychiatrist, and before they were released they had to really make a medical clearance.

C: Yes.

J: That's a far cry from, needless to say, "You don't have tomorrow off."

C: A long ways. Yeah.

J: Right? So where the individual was screened before he was released from the hospital at Sing-Sing, nobody even asked us how we felt. (Joe)

The nature of the after-care services did not visibly impact on the hostile attitude of the hostages. A survivor of Sing-Sing, where the most extensive and sophisticated after-care services were provided, was one of the angriest men.

J: I couldn't believe that people I worked for would do those kinds of things. But they did. Kind of like set us up. Let us take the fall. Then they tried to blame us for it!

C: A lot of anger . . .

J: A *lot* of anger. (Jerry)

One officer, seconds after release, fumed at and cursed the prison superintendent to his face. The superintendent had doubted the officer's information concerning who was still in the yard.

> I says, "You're full of shit." I says, "I just left the man. He *is* down there. Don't you people even know who the hell is in that yard?" I remember those remarks. I remember that . . . that . . . that . . . that . . . that instant, I wanted to smash him in the face. The superintendent! What the hell the good are they? Don't tell me I'm wrong! I'm the one who was down there, you weren't! They kept being adamant that that man was not there and he had been held hostage all day. And they had beat him in the kidneys! A lot of people were like those. . . . Why, it's the ivory tower again. (Brian)

One gets the feeling that his rage is larger than the specific trigger. He is railing against all those who don't understand—who may never understand—what he had just been through. The superintendent's misinformation becomes a metaphor for how remote this hostage victim feels from those around him—those others in their "ivory tower." It is only seconds after release, and the "second victimization" that Symonds (1980) speaks of has begun.

From the point of view of the hostages, the freedom came in a sudden and climactic way. The level of threat was high until the final moment. The arrival of freedom was a sudden, intense, sometimes overwhelming, experience. Anger toward authority surfaced immediately and found an enduring and prominent place in the psyche of the survivors.

4

Survival: Through the Years

Eleven of the men interviewed went through a hostage experience in 1970 or 1971. One officer was in the Sing-Sing riot that occurred in 1983. One wonders what meaning those traumatic events had in the lives of these men through the years. What challenges did they face? What problems did they have to overcome? In what ways do they believe they have changed?

GOING BACK

One of the first challenges faced was going back to work. For all but one of these men, this initially occurred in the same facility where they were terrorized. A survivor of Attica describes a grim and poignant scene days after the prison was retaken.

> I walked into the yard. This was when the prison . . . everything was still in the yard. All the tents, all the trenches, everything. The blood. Everything was still there. I walked over to where I was being held and there was my shoe laying there in the mud. And I looked up at one of the cell blocks, and that cell block had all the windows out onto the yard. There was two and three inmates to a cell because half the prison had been destroyed and they couldn't house them. They all looked

out at me, out of the windows. There was not one peep . . .
not a peep. (Richard)

The officer above tried to continue working at Attica but was haunted
by the memories.

R: I had a very difficult time dealing with Attica itself. I worked
at about six other prisons since then. Mediums, maximums,
minimums and I never had a problem in any of them. I have
been able to function fine. If I was to go back to Attica today,
I couldn't function there.

C: What happened when you did go back?

R: Well, it was kind of strange but I just, I wasn't rational. It was
like I was expecting things to come running at me and uh, I
would walk into areas and I would stop and find myself looking
down a hall waiting to see if a guy was coming down the hall
that I used to eat with . . . and he was killed. You know, that
type of thing would happen to me. I got back out. I couldn't
handle it. (Richard)

Some of the men who were interviewed were out of work for six
months; most went back fairly quickly, within days or a few weeks.
Although not interviewed for this study, there were survivors of each
uprising that never returned to corrections work. Those who went back
without much delay felt convinced that it was a good thing for them to
do.

Well, I knew I was nervous about going back. I was still
nervous about the whole situation, but I knew at the time
I went back that this place was locked up, locked in . . . I
felt that if I put it off over a long period of time, it would
be harder . . . I figured I had fourteen more years to go. You
can't be hiding for fourteen years. (Bill)

I think that it was important that I went right back to work.
(Richard)

Some of the officers didn't come back right away but stayed
out. My theory was the longer you stay out the worse you're
gonna be . . . So I went back to work the very next day. Some

of the officers that didn't had a little problem later on getting
back into it. You know, which you would. You know, the
longer you stay out from something like that. (Joe)

Going back, however, was not easy for most of these men. They
reported feeling very "nervous" and hypervigilant.

You were thinking that every minute there was something
was going to jump off. Every time that an inmate blew his
nose, you, you read something into that. In ordinary times,
you would never read anything into that. But in this, at this
point in time, you were reading all this stuff. (John)

TWELVE ANGRY MEN

The returning hostage survivors at Auburn, the first of the "mod-
ern" riots in New York State, were not met with much sensitivity
or compassion. Those who stayed home the next day received phone
calls from supervisors wondering why they were not at work. Back on
the job they were immediately assigned to posts with intense inmate
contact. They were threatened with dismissal if they balked. The anger
at administrators that was conceived in the hostage circle grew to rage
as the officers felt victimized once again. One officer admitted, "I was
a very uncooperative employee. I was very vocal. I was very active
in challenging administration policies and decisions. Yeah. That took
a while to get over . . . I think that a lot of administrators were very
tolerant because I was a pain in the ass" (Richard).

Survivors were "very bitter at the Department" (Bill) and found that
their feelings of doubt and mistrust toward the prison authorities persisted
over time.

Ever since then, I would always be concerned about the
people in power, like the commissioner, whether he was a
liberal or whether he was a staunch penologist or whether
the superintendent . . . I would always concern myself with
how strong he was, you know, because I knew at the time that
our deputy superintendent broke down, just . . . lost control of
himself on the day of the riot. He lost everything that day. And
so I was concerning myself later with who was going to run

the place in case a thing like this happened again. (Bill)

Anger and irritability sometimes became pervasive: "Well, I was always kind of like a mild-mannered type of an individual. But I could tell that I had lost most of that. I became more edgy. More aggressive and short-tempered" (Jerry).

No subjects identified themselves as having become physically abusive to family members. Many, however, spoke of other hostage survivors who abused their spouses or children after the riots. Alcohol abuse was often involved.

A RANGE OF PROBLEMS

Subjects reported that they experienced a number of problems after the riot, including marital and family problems. Some men experienced periods of sexual impotence. Others became sexually promiscuous.

> Many times my wife didn't even know where the hell I was . . . you know. I would go out and maybe wake up the next morning and find myself in Syracuse, wondering how the hell I got there. Sometimes, I will be honest with you, I might have been with a broad. Sometimes I was with no one. (John)

Most subjects reported post-riot symptoms that were suggestive of depression: sleep problems, fatigue, irritability, decreased libido, etc. Many identified themselves as having been through a period of depression. One man had come dangerously close to suicide—a tragedy averted by a frantic wife and the state police. The troopers found him sitting in his car staring at his gun.

Anxiety symptoms were frequently recognized in the months following the trauma. The men perceived themselves having become more nervous and fearful. They experienced waking flashbacks, dreams and hyperstartling. One man described what he endured for months after the riot.

> S: I didn't like anybody behind me. I slept fairly good but I slept . . . let's put it this way, I almost belted my sister when she came in the house and I was sleeping on the sofa. She surprised me and I got, I was ready to deck her. I don't think

really, I didn't really calm down for a while. Maybe on the outside, but not on the inside.

C: Not on the inside.

S: It took a while to calm that down. As far as dreaming the stuff, I dreamed for a while . . .

C: About the event?

S: The whole damn thing. (Steve)

Not surprisingly, they were affected at work.

You were certainly a hell of a lot more paranoid than you ever were in your life. At least some of us were. A simple fight between two inmates. We could see a riot starting. In your mind you could see a real big thing coming off of this. Okay? Up until a point in time that the riot went down, a simple fight was just a simple fight. (John)

FEAR AND AN ALTERED VIEW OF SELF

The experience of fear had an enduring significance for those men. It altered their perception of themselves.

Maybe it showed me a weakness in myself. It showed me that I was capable of fear. Something no man likes to face up to . . . and then when it is over, you say to yourself, I shouldn't have shown that fear. I shouldn't have shown that weakness in myself. (Richard)

The confrontation with their own fear and loss of control created feelings of vulnerability that were hard to shake. "Because I knew it could happen any minute for the next thirteen years, because things had completely changed and they run it. They can take that prison over at any time they want" (Philip).

Although there were intense feelings of inadequacy and vulnerability, subjects were not inclined toward extensive self-blame or guilt. This was found despite well-documented evidence that victims of rape or assault often blame themselves for their victimization (Burgess and Holmstrom, 1974). Three factors may have contributed to the lack of self-blame and guilt among this population.

1. The sheer magnitude of these events, which involved the actions of thousands of men, conveyed a sense of insignificance. How could a single individual, it could be reasoned, influence such a force? Although, perhaps, minimizing feelings of guilt, it is easy to imagine how the same factors could exaggerate feelings of helplessness. Indeed, such feelings were experienced in profound ways by the hostages.

2. In each riot there were several dozens of hostages taken. The number may have inhibited a perception of exclusive responsibility. It would be hard to imagine how all those officers could have made similar drastic errors at the same time.

3. All the subjects were low-ranking officers at the time of the riots. They had little authority or ability to affect policies or change strategies. Consistently, the hostages were not hesitant to rage against senior personnel who *were* in charge.

Some men reported anxiety symptoms that persist to this day; fear of crowds, general nervousness, etc. Most believed that the negative effects of the hostage-taking wore off within a few months to a year. At the same time, there were intriguing data that raised doubts about their self-assessment. A survivor of the Auburn riot, divorced a decade later, said that his former wife blamed their relationship problems on his hostage experience. Another man from Auburn was almost divorced several years after the riot. His wife, he reported, blamed their relationship problems on his emotional withdrawal and obsessive concentration on work after the riot. Still other subjects reported how they objected vehemently when their sons considered going into corrections work. It was, and still is, common for sons of correction officers to follow their fathers' occupational lead. Moreover, these families lived in communities where jobs in corrections were generally valued as steady, well-paid employment. It is noteworthy, then, that these hostage survivors reacted so negatively to the idea of their sons working in the prisons. Although the men interviewed often minimized or denied any continuing after-effects of their hostage experience, they retained their heightened sense of prisons as a dangerous place, a place not meant for loved ones.

P: They had a lot of guys, had their sons down there, making good money.

C: Yeah.

P: But I wouldn't, I don't know, I just . . .

C: You really discouraged it?

P: It would bother me to have them in there, working . . . I couldn't
 . . . I couldn't sleep if they were down there.

C: Couldn't sleep.

P: It was the best job in town, financially, the best job, anyway.
 (Philip)

There existed other indicators that the riots remained for some of these men a kind of partially healed wound, leaving them with some "unfinished business." This dramatically surfaced for David, a survivor of Auburn, who participated in the siege and assault on Attica. "The feelings that I had in Auburn weren't so severe as the feelings as I had in Attica looking in. In Auburn I was there. I was inside. There was a definite difference" (David).

Wesselius and DeSarno (1983) found that former hostages reported a reoccurrence of trauma symptoms when events occurred that resembled the earlier incident. Several men in this study reported feelings of identification and discomfort during certain highly publicized hostage-takings. For David, the similarity and proximity of the Attica incident made it hard to deal with. In his view, it was even harder than his own captivity experience.

In Attica I had many days to sit there and wonder about those people and what was going on through their minds out there knowing full well that I had faced and tasted a bit of it. But over a long period of time, what was it doing to their minds? How were they going to be affected . . . [It was] probably more devastating to me and, I think in the long run, turned out to be a hell of a lot more devastating than my actually being held hostage. (David)

The man seemed inexplicably drawn to the scene. He seemed to be fulfilling the often noted compulsion to repeat the trauma (A. Freud, 1974; S. Freud, 1920; Green, 1983; Terr, 1983). After arriving at Attica, he telephoned his wife. She angrily asked, "Why in hell are you there? Why you?" The question brought him up short. "I will never forget those words. Because I couldn't answer them. Why was I there? I didn't have to go to Attica. I could have declined it. But I had been through a hostage-taking. Why did my mind do these things? I hurt my wife very badly" (David).

If David's involvement at Attica was an attempt to integrate more fully his earlier trauma, it appeared to fail. After Attica, he admitted, he came close to a personal breakdown and a marital breakup. The Auburn riot remained what Shore (1986) termed an "incompletely mastered stressor event." This left David, perhaps, with a tendency toward increased symptomatology during and after similar events. Shore also postulated that well-mastered similar events would convey resilience. A stressor, therefore, would not automatically inoculate against nor sensitize a subject to future stress. Variables residing in the individual must be considered.

FROM VICTIMIZATION TO MASTERY

It is important to observe that hostage survivors interviewed in this study all returned to work in the prison system. One returned to work moments after his release. Others stayed home for six months. Some hostage survivors (not included in this study) never went back inside a prison. Some quit after a short time back on the job. As discussed in the methodology chapter, the men that were interviewed were not representative of all prison hostage survivors. The men who did not return to work could not be traced. They, however, have a story to tell—a story that may be different from the stories elicited in this study.

It is tempting to speculate that men who were able to return to work, function successfully and freely talk about their experience years later, were able to cope more effectively than some of their peers. The reaction of one man who refused to be interviewed supports such speculation: "It still bothers me too much. I don't know . . . No. I'm sorry. I can't talk about it."

Unfortunately, tempting speculation is not data, and little is truly known of the people who were not interviewed. It may be fair to assume, however, that the men who did participate in the study had integrated the traumatic experience in such a way that they could readily talk about it. They had dealt with the terror in a way that allowed them to return to work—often with the inmates who had terrorized them. This was no small achievement. It is hard to imagine parallels where victims and perpetrators would have such continuing contact—and even a kind of working relationship. The counseling and psychology literature does not often speak of courage as a motivator, but the word is difficult to avoid when considering these men.

CONTROL

Recovering from a traumatic experience is a task of some complexity and not explained by courage alone. One of the dominant features of this recovery was each victim's struggle to reestablish some sense of control over his life. His belief in his ability to determine his actions and his future was shattered. Left behind were feelings of helplessness, fear and vulnerability. It became crucial for these men to view themselves once again as having some control over their lives. Their sense of competence and self-worth depended on it. For the men in this study the struggle was a successful one. They confronted their demons and returned to the place of terror. With their fear conquered, their power returned.

> I thought to myself there is only one thing that can save a person in this type of situation—you, yourself, and your ability to keep your wits. You, yourself, to prevent it from happening through whatever it takes . . .
>
> Today I take a chance of being a hostage at any given moment. It doesn't bother me. I pretty much . . . I pretty much feel I will never be taken hostage through my own ability to control the environment around me . . . (Brian)

This man was able to reassert his authority in a crucial area of his environment. This was a key challenge that all of the men faced and, eventually, met. One subject, John, was initially defeated by the challenge. After four weeks out of work, he returned to the prison and, despite administrator reluctance, he was assigned to his old post—one that was a high-risk location.

J: They thought it best to put me on a different job. I was pretty adamant about it. It was like, I had to prove something. So after a couple of days discussion, the hard-headed me finally won out and went back to my old job. I was down in my old job. It was . . . it was . . . uh . . . it was tough. But I thought that was the only way I was going to lick it.

C: What made it tough for you?

J: Being back on the job, in the same place the riot took place. The same place that I had gotten beat up three or four or five different times. (John)

In the aftermath of the riot, no talking was allowed as inmates moved through the corridors and the blocks. The groups of quiet inmates harkened back to the pregnant silence before the riot.

J: There was no talking. No noise. No noise.

C: The silence.

J: Because you were thinking that every minute there was something was going to jump off. The silence.

C: Silence.

J: The silence. And I lasted through the silence for about close to a week. And I couldn't handle it.

C: What did it do to you?

J: Well, it would just get to you. You would become very paranoid. You'd think something was going to kick off any minute. Every time an inmate blew his nose, you, you would read something into that. In ordinary times, you would never read anything into that . . . I just told the Sergeant that I couldn't cut it. I got to go up front. I got to get out of here.

C: Had to leave.

J: And he got another officer. I went up front and talked to the Deputy Superintendent for a minute. And a . . . a . . . a . . . and that got to me. When they were able to get to me again [as they did during the riot]. That got to me too.

C: Yeah.

J: Bothered me a great deal. (John)

John was out for several more months. He became heavily involved with alcohol and valium. He engaged in extra-marital affairs. He had problems with drunken driving and had even been arrested and briefly jailed for assault—the ultimate humiliation for a correction officer. "Everything seemed to be going down, down. Everything seemed to be going down. Nothing was right. You know, everything was based. So one night I decided that . . . I thought maybe I ought to kill myself" (John).

On the edge of suicide, the deeply troubled man was picked up by the police and returned home. In the subsequent soul searching, there occurred a realization—and a new commitment to life.

> Maybe I was on the brink. I don't know . . . I just said, man, you have got to stop. You have *got* to stop it. You are ruining everyone in your family's life and along with [it] your own. You are really hurting them bad. So I tried to get my act together. Go back to work.
>
> I was somewhat apprehensive about going back . . . uh . . . I didn't feel good. After about two weeks, three weeks, four weeks, the whole Goddamn thing left me. I just hung in there and everything left me. The feeling of apprehension . . . any paranoia I had had just . . . I was back in the ball game! (John)

In John's second confrontation with his demons, he was triumphant. His sense of control, his ability to make his own choices had returned. The renewed power can be heard in the language he used to describe the change in himself. "I pulled everything in because it was either do or die. You either are going to lick it or you weren't going to lick it. that is the bottom line. Either you did or you didn't. And I made up my mind I had to" (John).

John's struggle warrants closer inspection for several reasons. It may very well be a more intense and more prolonged version of the path followed by other survivors. It is a road leading to the essential, existential choice: What will I make of myself? Some others had an easier time of it, but the process itself was similar. There was a reoccurring theme of man making critical decisions.

> From that point on I decided . . . I'm going to help myself. (Brian)

> You can't really tell people how to handle yourself afterwards, how to cope with your experience, 'cause they have to do it themselves, but . . . you just got to watch your step, that's all. Don't get yourself in a position where you don't want to be. Don't let it affect your mind . . . like it can. Don't go running in bars and . . . you know. You ain't getting it out that way, because it's not the answer. Try to keep yourself in control

after, which is an easy thing to say, but you've got to do it. (Bill)

Each one of us had to deal with it in our own way, each one of us. Maybe a man had a religion that gave him strength. Maybe he . . . he had a family that he wanted to project a good image to. That was my case. Maybe he could sit down and was still rational enough to say to himself, "I got a lot of life left. I got to decide right now, how I am going to provide for my family? If I am going to continue in this field, am I going to make it? And if I can't, I got to, I got to take another direction." And some of us would. I would have considered that an inadequacy in me . . . a . . . a . . . unmasculine. I had to prove something to myself by staying there. (Richard)

John and the others, at different points, asked themselves similar questions and ended up making similar choices. However, the painful, and almost deadly, aftermath of the riot for John may offer a window into experiences of other survivors—those who were not able to rebuild their lives so fully. In John's story, there may be a marker for a path taken by other hostage survivors. Although the subjects were invited to talk about themselves, they sometimes discussed their friends. They talked in quiet tones about the man who "ate his gun" and others who started to beat their children or spouse. Subjects talked about men who couldn't maintain steady employment, who just seemed to lose the ability to cope with life. "You saw a lot of change in character in people is what you saw. They became the opposite of what they were in many cases" (Richard).

Subjects were non-judgmental toward the men who did not do so well. They talked with compassion, and even sadness, about their colleagues who suffered so much. As one man put it, "I, maybe, have become a little more sensitive to human frailty" (Richard).

These men found that returning to correction work was an important part of their efforts to master their trauma experience. They did not, interestingly, perceive that as an answer for everyone. There was strong consensus that each man must privately decide what kind of world he would make for himself.

Different reasons for different people. No one, no two people have the same reason for continuing on with the Department or for getting out and going . . . other ways. I . . . some of my good friends quit the day after the prison was taken back and they never went back in there. They went to Montana, Colorado and California and ah . . . yep, yep . . . not any employment, not anything. They just went. And that is really, those were the most successful people surprisingly enough . . . The ones that said "I got a father-in-law that can give me a job in Florida. I will go down there and work for him" didn't seem to make out. You would always see them drifting back. But the guy that just said, "To hell with it all. I'm going. I don't give a shit if I don't have ten cents in my pocket tomorrow. I'm never going back in that jail." They loaded everything they owned in their car and left. And I did have some friends that did this. They made out great. These people were like pioneers. They went out and they, they just, whatever they did, they committed themselves to it very intensely and they were a success. (Richard)

It is intriguing that, whether talking about themselves or perceived successful coping in others, subjects saw relying on oneself and that "pioneer spirit" as a decisive element of mastering their experience. It was in the lonely process of looking at themselves with stark honesty, a self with fears and weaknesses revealed, that they found the resources to build a new identity, a new life. For, indeed, they were forever changed. "Let's put it this way. I think once you consider yourself dead and got a second chance, you look at things a little bit differently" (Steve).

BEYOND MASTERY: NEW MEANING

As they returned their lives to some degree of normalcy, some survivors integrated their experiences in a way that allowed them to grow as individuals—to become more than they used to be.

I think I tried to live life and make it a little fuller after that . . . appreciate it more . . . I think it affected me in a way that you cope better with things. You learn to cope with things better. I think I'm always saying now, "Now don't get excited," you know. Try to keep your calm or not raise your voice . . . try to maintain a level of coolness, you know? Before [the riot] I would blow off steam a lot sometimes . . . but now, I say to myself, calm down, you know. You can handle things a different way. (Bill)

Although the words suggest a significant internal process of attitude change, they are spoken with authentic simplicity:

> I said to myself, "When I get out of here, if I make it out," I said, when I was in the [prison] yard, sitting there thinking, "I live for today and forget about tomorrow" . . . You know, best not go out and buy a new Cadillac and a new beautiful home you can't afford. But every year since then or every two or three years I have bought a new car and we have gone on trips and everything. So I got a feeling of, "Hey, I'm gonna live today." Because it might have ended right there. (Joe)

> I feel in a way that you look at things a little more. You do a little bit more of the things that you enjoy doing (Steve).

The words of these men echo the findings of Thompson (1985) in her study of individuals whose homes had been destroyed by fire. Survivors who found some positive way to re-evaluate their loss were found to be able to cope more effectively. In addition to other strategies, they found some positive side effects to their experience. Families were brought closer together; victims were buoyed by the support and caring of neighbors and friends. They also spoke of being made more aware of the preciousness of life in a way that routine events cannot convey.

Some of the men in this study were active in training crisis management teams for the Department. The former hostages felt that it was important for these teams to understand how a hostage subjectively feels during and after the riot. In doing this training, they would meet with thirty or forty people, their colleagues, and publicly talk of intimate things. They would talk of sexual problems and alcohol abuse, fear and shame. They would talk of the struggle and the long road back. They made their pain meaningful by making it an instrument to help others. David, now a senior officer and commander of hundreds of men and women, described, with tears and a halting voice, what it meant to him. "I get emotional when I think about it . . . I do it because I want to help somebody else. I a . . . a . . . if I can help somebody, even if I don't know him, I can relate to him" (Ron).

These men have intuitively found the value of what Frankl (1963) called *dereflection*—getting away from the endless rumination about the sources of one's anxiety and depression. Instead they directed their attention to the healthier parts of their personalities and focused on the meaningful things they could do and the contributions they could make. It is as if they found their own path to Yalom's (1980) concept of engagement—finding something that captures their attention and pursuing it with passion. He held that in order to fill the void left by losses in one's life, it is not necessary to discover the elusive, ultimate meaning of life. According to Yalom's existential framework, it is up to each man and woman to invent his or her own meaning in the present moment.

HELPLESSNESS VERSUS COMPETENCE

Reasserting his sense of personal power and competence was extremely important to the hostage after he left captivity. At the shorter, and somewhat less violent riot in Auburn, some went back to work immediately or the very next day. Years later, they still believed that it was the very best thing that they could have done for themselves.

Even during the chaos and terror of the riots, men strived to take control in moving and remarkable ways. One man fully believed that he was going to die at the hands of the inmates who were beating him mercilessly. By any objective standard, he was in a totally helpless position. Nevertheless, he took control, not of the situation, but of himself. Sure he was going to die, but he would *choose* to die with dignity. He would give his sons the gift of a father they could always remember with pride. Another officer, a lieutenant, given his freedom and told to leave, would not budge from the hostage circle. He defiantly said he would stay until all of "his men" were free.

These hostages, during captivity and later, managed to reassert a degree of command over their destiny. Instead of remaining totally passive and helpless, they seized opportunities they could find to reaffirm their lost power.

Maddi and Kobasa (1984) identified a sense of control as an important element in what they described as "hardiness." They found that people who resisted stress, who did not succumb to crises by becoming ill, operated with the belief that they could exert control over events. Johnson and Savarson (1978) found that negative life events were significantly related to anxiety and depression, but the relationship only held for subjects with an externally oriented locus of control.

Laboratory research on learned helplessness further supports this conclusion (Seligman, 1975). Animals and humans, after being persuaded in one phase of the experiment that they could not control aversive stimuli, made no attempt to change the situation even after control was restored. These studies support the view that people are more adversely affected by life stress if they perceive themselves as having little control over their environment.

A less discussed but, perhaps, equally important aspect of Seligman's research is the finding that one-third of the dogs did not show the typical performance decrements and learned helplessness features. He did not know if this resilience was a genetic or learned trait, but it documented that some organisms successfully adapt to aversive stimuli that renders others passive and helpless.

For the survivors who participated in this study, there seemed to be three factors that mediated their successful adjustment after their trauma.

1. Personal control. As described by Flannery (1987) personal control is taken to have two components: internal control and a set of situation specific skills. Persons who see themselves as at the mercy of outside circumstances feel helpless and have less adaptive ability. Those with an internal locus of control are able to exert some mastery over their lives. Secondly, specific skills are needed to be effective in specific situations. Prior experience and the acquisition of certain skills in coping with problems has been found to reduce anxiety and depression and enhance a sense of personal mastery (Bandura, 1977; Flannery, 1986).

2. Task involvement. Task involvement signifies being absorbed in a task and guided by what the task requires. Former hostages selected tasks that were personally meaningful: training other officers, changing the system, professionalizing their jobs, etc. Also referred to as committed (Flannery, 1987) or industrious (Vaillant and Vaillant, 1981), these people have a belief system that precludes feelings of helplessness.

3. Social supports. Hostages used the social supports of other people as a buffer in dealing with the post-riot stress in their lives. Personal relationships provided companionship, empathic listening, information and instrumental help in solving problems.

SUMMARY

It was a poignant and difficult challenge for some, but all of the interviewed hostages went back to work. It was, perhaps, their most important step in achieving mastery over their trauma. They literally stepped back into control, reasserting their authority over themselves and the world around them.

Survivors experienced a range of problems and emotions after their return to freedom. The most prominent and persistent emotion was anger. Their rage was most strongly directed toward their own superiors. In their perception, it was prison officials who mismanaged events that led to the riots and then failed to win the freedom of the captives in a timely way.

Fear and helplessness during the riot left a legacy for the survivors of a changed self-image and diminished self-confidence. Instead of their vision of themselves as tough, unafraid, and in control, they were given a glimpse of themselves as vulnerable, terrified, and helpless. They struggled to re-establish a sense of control and coherence in their lives. Involvement with meaningful work and closeness to social supports aided this process.

Nevertheless, things were different. Prisons seemed more dangerous than before. Then again, life was also more valuable and more meaningful. If they were more nervous, they were also more sensitive and tolerant of others. Psychologists may debate the nature of the changes, but it seems inarguable that they were forever changed.

5

Hostage Victims and the Counseling Profession: Implications and Recommendations

The men who participated in this study took some psychological risks to do so. Yet after their initial mistrust, they spoke openly and willingly of terrible experiences and painful memories. Their public front, hardened by years in the prisons, softened as they shared their feelings and exposed their frailties. The stories they told left the researcher with the conviction that these men have an important message. The message is for psychologists, counselors and others who would be helpers to those who have suffered the trauma of being taken hostage in a prison. Moreover, their message may have implications beyond helping someone deal with the trauma of captivity. In drug research it is common to use extraordinarily high doses of a substance with laboratory animals so that even subtle effects may be observed. Similarly, it is possible that the incredibly intense stress of a hostage experience may surface reactions that occur in other forms of victimization.

In any event, the data gathered in this study contains treatment implications along five dimensions: (1) information and education; (2) individual differences; (3) support systems; (4) dealing with competence and control issues; and (5) individual and group counseling with victims.

INFORMATION AND EDUCATION

One way to help survivors is to normalize the recovery process. Victims typically know very little about what a traumatic experience can do to a person. Letting them know that certain reactions are normal, that the process is somewhat predictable, can be very reassuring.

A victimization experience may be as profound as bereavement, but there are few social and cultural mechanisms in place to affirm, guide and support the victim as he recovers. If a correction officer's spouse died, he would not have been expected to return to work the next day. On the contrary, there would be an outpouring of support, rituals to give structure to his time and both formal and informal permission to grieve, to be affected by his loss. The hurt or loss to hostage victims is still, at times, not fully recognized unless there is a physical injury. As one man put it, "They said we were cry-babies" (Ron). The victims' sense of inadequacy was magnified because they could not easily put the experience behind them.

It is possible to be both honest and hopeful in providing to victims information about traumatic stress reactions. If the problems are identified, then there is an increased opportunity to seek out the most adaptive, least destructive ways of living through it and mastering it.

INDIVIDUAL DIFFERENCES

It would be convenient to be able to reduce the hostage response into a single pattern. While similarities do exist, there are also many differences. Ignoring those differences would be offensive to the victims and an obstacle to providing effective services. Subjects repeatedly made the point that the experience affected everyone differently.

> I don't know anyway to explain it, but it doesn't affect everyone the same. (John)

> And how one person can deal with it and another not, you know, I don't know. Why does one man catch the flu and another not catch it? (Richard)

> Everybody sees different. If we were all alike, what a hell of a world we would have. No, everybody has their own thought process. Everybody has their own souls and their own minds. (Brian)

The meaning that an event for a person is highly subjective. One hostage who experienced fear regarded it as a normal, even healthy reaction to a threatening situation. For another man it meant a devastating loss of identity and self-esteem. Because people are different in the way they perceive and process events, those differences need to be acknowledged and respected.

SUPPORT SYSTEMS

Hostage survivors sought support among their natural support groups: family, other survivors, other co-workers, barroom and neighborhood friends. Events would be talked about over and over again as the experience was processed and given meaning by each individual. Most hostages had spent considerable time in their respective communities and had strong support there. On the other hand, a survivor of the Sing-Sing riot had only been in Ossining one month and felt the loneliness acutely. "It was kind of rough because, you know, after everybody left, you were there all by yourself and stuff and I was the only one . . . I had to come home by myself" (Jerry).

As discussed earlier, research has shown a link between the strength of support systems and an individual's emotional and physical resilience under stress. A person's support system itself, however, may need support. For instance, a victim's family may have become indirect victims. Their world also has been shaken; they, too, have been terrified. Further, they have had little experience in responding to the needs of a trauma victim. Acknowledging their pain, affirming their role as supports and, once again, sharing information about the recovery process may enhance the support function of family or co-workers.

Furthermore, Dean and Lin (1977) have suggested that training in the social skills needed to get help from friends, relatives and the community when stress reaches high levels might protect a significant number of individuals from personal difficulties. Even with the growing sophistication about victim needs, social support issues are often overlooked.

Social support needs to be considered in the context of the victim's need to see himself once again as competent and self-reliant. Subjects frequently spoke about their belief that they needed, ultimately, to do it on their own. It was perceived as "really just a case of coming to grips with it yourself" (John). It would be important, at least for this population of survivors, not to diminish this perception of personal power by overemphasizing the need for support.

Reliance on others and self-reliance may not be incompatible. In related research, it has been found that adults who are self-reliant, adept at coping with stress, and able to maintain a positive attitude in the face of challenges usually had childhoods marked by the personal security that goes along with warm relationships and shared experiences (Petersen & Spiga, 1982). Rather than necessarily promoting dependency, supportive relationships may empower individuals to cope more effectively and independently.

COMPETENCE AND CONTROL

Survivors of a hostage-taking or other victimization experience need to be approached as competent, capable human beings. They should be given control over their lives once again, starting with the basics: where to sit, what to eat or drink, to rest or to talk, etc. In most cases they could be affirmed for enduring under extraordinary circumstances. Courage could be acknowledged not because they were unafraid but because they managed despite their fear. Former hostages should be encouraged to resume involvement in usual home, work and community activities as soon as they feel ready.

Victims need help in moving from chaos to order, from helplessness to control. Re-establishing the familiar and dependable routines of everyday life can help restore their trust in life's predictability. Survivors should be further encouraged to take initiative: to act on their problems, to do something productive and to structure their time. They may need, however, to be reminded to go easy on themselves and not expect immediate successes or perfect solutions. These things may help the victims truly to become survivors and regain their sense of personal power that had been violently wrested from them.

INDIVIDUAL AND GROUP TREATMENT

In addition to managing the environmental and institutional response to victims, mental health professionals also can be helpful in more direct ways. The clinician, however, first must become accessible and build credibility with the victims. Persons disorganized by traumatic shock may not be able to take much initiative in getting help. Moreover, because a victimization experience often leaves a person feeling alienated and misunderstood, a counselor should be able to demonstrate that he can understand and does have some helpful expertise.

A clinician can work to make many feelings seem less overwhelming by encouraging the person to work through the feelings one step at a time rather than all at once. Exercise and relaxation strategies can be suggested to help manage tension or anxiety. Referrals for medication can be made as appropriate. Victims can be guided to restoring control and self-reliance by helping them focus on tasks and make realistic plans to deal with challenges. Trauma-related interpersonal problems may benefit from appropriate interpretation and counseling.

Spiegel (1988) devised a therapeutic approach for trauma survivors that he neatly summarized as a series of "eight C's." First the importance of the traumatic event is *confronted*. Then the clinician and client attempt to form a *condensation* of the traumatic event: a scene or memory that can represent the horror of the event that can be faced. Then there may be a phase characterized by *confession*, in which the survivor tests the therapist's acceptance and resilience. This is followed by *consolation* and then an effort to make feelings of pain, shame and fear more *conscious*. At this point, *concentration* is useful to limit the scope of the loss, helping the client to grieve, but at a pace he or she can handle. At this stage of transition, a sense of *control* is vital and allows the individual to achieve a greater sense of *congruence*, feeling like "an integrated person who has been able to face and bear a period of tragedy and incorporate it into the flow of life" (Spiegel, 1988, p. 32).

Perhaps the most challenging aspect of working with survivors of hostage-takings, and probably other profound trauma as well, is helping the survivors restore or reaffirm some sense of purpose or meaning in their lives. Parsons (1990) believed that post-traumatic demoralization can be overcome, but the survivor must be motivated and committed.

> He or she must be willing to risk everything; for nothing less will do. The survivor must fight for his or her own existence and psychological well-being. Since everyone is responsible for the life he or she has been given, the patient must be willing to demonstrate courage. (p. 26)

The men in this study, especially the ones who seemed to be happiest and most fulfilled, found the courage—something to commit themselves to. Like the POWs who came home from Vietnam and went into Survival Training (Segal, 1986), some of the survivors turned their suffering into an opportunity to help others. They became involved in hostage training for the Department of Correctional Services. Others rededicated themselves to their chosen profession. They sought and gained promotions and worked to change and improve the Department from within. Still others started their own businesses or recommitted themselves to family life. Observations by Segal (1986) suggested that these were not isolated cases. Data from Iranian hostages, American veterans and holocaust survivors point to the importance of trying to find some meaning in the madness, giving it some purpose. Yalom (1980) called it "engagement," finding something that captures our attention and then pursuing it passionately.

One way of encouraging engagement is with groups. Yalom (1980) claimed that it is important to get stress-ridden individuals to stop thinking about themselves and to start thinking of others. He found group work to be a good vehicle to achieve this. In a group, self-serving behavior is readily apparent and inevitably became an issue among group members. Moreover, compassionate and supportive behavior is usually acknowledged and reinforced. Segal (1986) has advocated for the value of victim self-help groups. Reissman (1965) observed that such groups can do more than help one find personal meaning in helping others. He concluded that when people join together with others to deal with common problems, then they were exercising control over some aspect of their lives. The result is a renewed sense of empowerment. Power and purpose come together to help the victim become victor.

FUTURE RESEARCH

This study contributes to a growing literature on victims of violence and trauma. One of the more unique aspects of the research is its long-term perspective. Few studies have examined the ramifications of hostage victimization years or decades later. With its qualitative approach, this work has tried to go deeper than the reporting of the frequency and incidence of symptoms. It also has endeavored to raise questions for future research on hostage victims in various settings.

This study did not solicit information directly from the family members of the hostages. The men, however, spoke about their families as having been very involved in events during and after the riots. Issues surfaced that point to some intriguing questions for future research.

1. To what extent were family members indirectly victimized and affected by the extraordinary danger experienced by their loved ones?

2. How were family relationships affected by the trauma and its aftermath? How were interpersonal problems handled and with what result?

3. What perspective did close family members, parents, wives and children, have toward the primary victim and his needs, problems, strengths, etc.?

There are other ways in which to extend the research conducted in this study. With the necessary funding and the active support of the involved institutions, one might be able to interview the hostage survivors who did not return to work in the prisons. Although they live in various places around the country and would be difficult to trace, these men probably would have a different point of view than the men who continued to work with inmates. For the subjects in this study, going to work meant an enhanced sense of mastery and control. It would be interesting to know how the men who made different choices dealt with this and other challenges.

Retrospective studies of other hostage populations would further enrich our understanding of this phenomenon and its impact on human beings. Many different people take hostages for many different reasons: bank robbers trying to arrange their freedom, terrorists trying to make a statement, psychotics trying to accomplish something only they understand. Hostages may be in higher risk occupations such as correction officers, diplomats, psychiatric hospital staff or airline crews. They may simply be cab drivers or secretaries with very bad luck. Victims may be men, women, highly educated, blue collar workers, in America or abroad, alone or with a plane-load of people. Although certain elements of a hostage experience are consistent—victims are taken captive and held under the threat of violence in exchange for certain goods or services— the people and the circumstances involved may be quite different. In order for mental health professionals to be respectful of group and individual differences, we need further research to help us understand the meaning of the event for different populations of victims.

SUMMARY

Given this study's focus on hostage victims, it is tempting to consider it in the context of the growing body of research on terrorism. To the extent in which elements of a hostage experience may be universal (helplessness, violence or the threat of violence, isolation, fear, etc.) such a comparison is appropriate. Aspects of the experience very well may be similar for correction officers and international hostage victims. Clearly, however, prison riots also are different from other hostage events in a number of (perhaps important) ways: an identified location with defined and controlled perimeters, the large number of hostage-takers with variable power relationships among sub-groups, the power reversal that occurs, prior relationships among many of the participants, and the degree of similarity among the victims.

It is not the intent of this book to examine the specific differences that exist between prison riots and terrorist incidents. This book focuses on the phenomenological experience of victims more than the sociological phenomena in which they occur. It is a study of terrified people rather than a study of "terrorism." As such, the study is best placed in the context of victimization research. The framework for this research was built in Chapter 1 and Chapter 2. The data found a comfortable fit within this structure and, hopefully, gave it more clarity. The perspective for understanding victimization was well summarized by Janoff-Bulman and Frieze (1983):

> Although specific victimizations may differ, there appears to be common psychological responses across a wide variety of victims. It is proposed that victims' psychological distress is largely due to the shattering of basic assumptions held about themselves and their world. Three assumptions that change as result of victimization are: 1) the belief in personal invulnerability; 2) the perception of the world as meaningful; and 3) the view of the self as positive. (p. 1)

This book has examined how hostage victims perceive their victimization and how they go about the task of rebuilding their assumptive world. In sharing the intimate details of this process, the hostage survivors have allowed us to be close observers in their efforts to redefine their world and themselves. They have served to expose the internal and external forces that have helped or hindered their efforts. In shedding more light on the phenomena of victimization, this research has attempted to contribute to the empirical knowledge of this area. In deepening our understanding of the needs of victims and survivors, it is my hope that this book has enhanced the ability of the mental health profession and society to be of service.

Appendix A

Sample Interview

INTERVIEW WITH DAVID

Field Notes:
I am about to interview Lieutenant ———. He was a hostage at the Auburn riot in 1970. I was referred to Lieutenant ——— by ——— and ———, who were also hostages at the Auburn riot. Lieutenant ——— is currently working at the ——— Correctional Facility. He rooms there with three other officers from ——— and on weekends commutes back to his home in Auburn. Unlike some others who have agreed reluctantly to speak with me, Lieutenant ——— has seemed rather eager to talk about his experience. Some ambiguous comments that he has made, as well as his tone during our telephone conversations, brief though they were, suggest that he has much to tell me. My impression is that he is hinting that the hostage experience has affected him rather profoundly. It is a cool, rather gray day in the upstate New York area, and I will be meeting Lieutenant ——— in his apartment in ———, New York, which is located near ———.

Campbell: I wonder if, just by way of putting it in context, you might describe your perceptions, your recollections of the event itself, kind of what led up to it, what happened before it and during it.

David: Uh . . . my first contact of any kind of a hostage situation happened in the fall of 1970 at Auburn Correctional Facility. I was a guard at the time. For rhyme or reason as to why in that specific spot I was not in my normal work station, which was not my pattern. We had had trouble a couple of days prior to that and they thought that it pretty much was under control. It had surfaced, I believe, on a Wednesday morning. It had surfaced in the effect that people, inmates, took the opportunity to express their feelings. It was based on Muslim's and the Muslim religion faction at that point in time the State did not recognize.

C: Yes.

D: Uh, based on that, these people then influenced many. Few influenced many in that respect because a prison system runs with many being controlled by a few.

C: I see.

D: Guards over inmates.

C: Okay.

D: Uh, there were breakdowns for a couple of days in that control process by trained professionals, which would be the Officer and the Supervisor. They broke down to a point where a certain few were able to take the initiative. It happened in the morning . . . a Wednesday morning. There was time that was given for these people to build up their power base, by that I mean . . . [Brief interruption]

C: Okay. Where were we? You were talking about that morning, Wednesday morning.

D: All right. I was talking about why we got to the point we got to. But I would have to say that these people have gained the importance of being able to control many. They actually basically took it away from us. Not because we really let them because this other chain of command took control. Certain decisions were being made. This is the first time something like this had surfaced in the State of New York, probably since the riots in 1929 which were a vast difference.

C: Yes.

D: Different type of . . . had a lot chronology.

C: Yeah.

D: In any event, these people were able to, over a period of time that morning, effectively keep inmates from going over to the shop areas . . . effectively controlled the inmate population. We had lost control. We weren't trained in any kind of these situations. They were all brand new experiences to the Administrative staff.

C: Hmm.

D: And this went on for a number of hours in the morning until finally what had taken place, these people had gained in importance in their mind that they were infallible; that they could do what they wanted to do and were free to get away with certain things. It just kept building, you know. I later on likened it in a psychology class to the trained animal being trained to a certain point and then allowing to go beyond that point and then causing chaos. They thought they were invincible from the first part. I don't have the technical language that a psychologist probably would. In any event, as the morning wore on, various parts of the institution that was runnable to the inmates was being commanded by the inmates. They took over our yard post in the yard. They took over our speaker, loudspeaker systems, and we jammed them from the inside. And then they proceeded to come in and take command away from the various blocks to release inmates that were under some kind of Administrative restriction. Either ordered us to do it, or they themselves took the keys and released, as we call it, their "brothers" out of Keeplock for various things that had taken place the last couple of days for leading and abetting some of this. These people were then released to the yard. Then they took over various blocks. Then they started taking hostages. They started taking people and they rapidly took them out of our control centers. They took them out of the various blocks. Over a period of time they were mixed in together and the syndrome called the "Hostage Circle" was born—in Auburn. Later carried on into Attica. The "Hostage Circle" had everybody in a large circle.

C: What do you recall the purpose of the circle was?

D: I haven't the slightest idea other than the fact that they would be centrally located, centrally controlled. You would have guards behind you and you would be facing each other across this large circle.

C: Uh huh.

D: If they wanted to talk to you, then they could stand in the center and talk to the whole by just turning around a little bit. It was a gathering— the way they got it just happened to develop into a circle. Like the old wagon train.

C: Yeah. Where were you as this started?

D: I was in one of the blocks and there were various things that took place that were administratively designed at that time that I am not going to disclose.

C: Okay.

D: In any event, at a certain point in time, the action came on me. I was told later that I came close to getting an axe handle in the head and only because I slipped down some steps at the time did that miss my head. I suppose at that point I might, I came close to being a physical subject. I wasn't really physically abused in this thing. My mind was a little abused before it got over with. [Laughter] I was taken hostage at approximately 10:30 or I was grabbed at approximately 10:30 and then the "Hostage Circle" born probably half hour to forty-five minutes later. And I was herded with approximately 50 of us altogether by the time noon rolled around. And they were all in this specific "Hostage Circle." Umm . . . I had tried to secure a block, I suppose. I had tried to yet still be the authoritive figure.

C: Yeah.

D: And I think that is the reason why someone took a swing at me with an axe handle from behind as I went down some steps. As I stepped down these steps leading out of the area, that is when the axe handle missed me—swished across the top of my head. I didn't realize it then. Other inmates that knew me, had worked for me in the kitchen area told me that how close it had come afterwards. You know, the next day or so. I was then herded out into the yard, run out in to the yard. I was moving but a few others were being run from some place else so it wasn't one person chasing you and taking a swing at you. That just happened once, a quick swing at the entrance of the block area.

C: Yeah.

D: I arrived into the so-called group in the center. Then it was just a mass of people. And they moved us around from there down the other end of the yard, way down to the other end of the yard. I don't know why, but a gas grenade was thrown in to the yard at that time. I watched a man, an older guard, to the left of me get clobbered in the shoulder. I don't know why. They just took the first guy and they swung at him because the gas grenade had come down in the yard and we all got gassed at that point. Swung right into us. Uh . . . I remember stepping from the corner, I was sort of in the corner. We were like in two lines into an L-shaped corner. And I remember stepping out of the corner reacting to him being hit. And I got grabbed. I was taken and grabbed by the shirt and I guess, I guess we had break-away ties. It is the only thing I can vividly remember. The break-away tie didn't work. [Laughter] It stayed around my neck and they grabbed and were choking me a little bit. And of course I was gassed and I was crying a little from the gas and what not. And then somebody played around with, I guess two or three of them, played around with me and they led me up between a back stop and a cage area. They hauled me up to the center of that space, one on each side of me, and somebody behind me, more behind me choking me or hanging on to me. And somebody had something in my stomach. I assume it was some kind of shank. I never did see it. It did prick me. It did leave the little spot of blood on my shirt so it was something sharp. And they were yelling out words of the nature of, "The next time you shoot, the next time you do something, whatever you do, this blue belly gets it," that type of thing. The word "blue belly" was used. I vividly remember that word. What went through my mind at that point in time is gone. I haven't the slightest idea if I had fear, if I had uh . . . I can't remember any kind of a feeling at that point, other than the fact of the events that were vivid around me. Of course nothing else was thrown. At that point in time I can't remember if they brought the people over to me or took me back or what not. But within moments we were all herded back up in to the center of the yard again. This is the reason we went out in the open. They had us back in the corner and they were trapped back there with us. I think that that is what brought out the "Hostage Circle."

C: I see.

D: It was a hostage type situation in the middle of an open area, where they could control. They dragged benches over and they formed this huge circle and then the Officers were forced to sit down on that bench. At that point in time things started quieting down. We weren't moved again. We stayed on that bench until we were ultimately released. Umm . . . a year later that same type of bench, the facing each other effect, was utilized at Attica. And I witnessed that.

C: You did?

D: From the outside.

C: Ah.

D: So that was whatever was born on that bench in Auburn was carried out with the same type of people pulling the same type of thing for whatever reason in Attica.

C: Yeah.

D: They are related—contrary to popular belief. They are related. And I was an insider and witnessed various people doing various things in both areas.

C: Yeah.

D: One from the inside and one from the outside looking in.

C: Both perspectives, really.

D: And uh . . . I have a feeling that what I remember of it, the feelings that I had in Auburn weren't as severe as the feelings as I had in Attica looking in. In Auburn I was there. I was inside. There was a definite difference. I was on both sides of this fence. In Auburn, it was more of a feeling as to, "Why am I here?" and "What is this all about?" and "Can this really be happening?" that type thing. As in Attica, it was looking in and some of the thoughts were, "My God, what are those people going through out there?"

C: Hm.

D: "What are their minds being subjected to?" Knowing what had basically gone through my mind in a short period of time. In Attica, it lasted for four days being held hostage.

C: Yeah.

D: I was only held hostage for approximately five hours.

C: Five hours.

D: Five to six hours, that they actually held me, being told what to do by somebody else other than my wife, or my superiors. [Laughter] So in Attica I had many days to sit there and wonder about those people and what was going through their minds out there knowing full well that I had faced and tasted a bit of it. But over a long period of time, what was it doing to their minds? How were they going to be affected? These are the thought patterns that ran through my mind in Attica.

C: Sure.

D: Which are probably more devastating to me and I think in the long run turned out to be a hell of a lot more devastating than my actually being held hostage.

C: Really?

D: Yeah.

C: You were identifying with the men inside.

D: Maybe because of the fact that I live in what they call a semi-rough world and a semi-dangerous world. Some people think we're nuts to live in it. To me it is perfectly normal. Today I run a discipline system, we control the discipline of an institution through our proceedings. And I have no problems about handing out punishments and walking around with those same people. I have no fears of that. I do it day in and day out. Let's face it. I have been doing it for 31 years. I have been on the job for close to 31 years. I have no intention of retiring. I have no fear of my job. I have no other pursuits I'd like to go to at this point in time, subject to change because I am in the retirable age. So the options are mine.

C: Yeah.

D: But the . . . being held hostage didn't really scare me that much. For some reason it didn't have that awful shaking and fear. Yet I saw others do that.

C: Saw others . . . hostages?

D: Now, you better believe my knees were shaking. I mean, I'm not, I'm saying my mind pattern was not my, you know . . . I'm scared, yes. But my pattern isn't to be so scared that I'd become paranoid and become useless.

C: Yeah.

D: My mind did an awful lot of things out there. As I said, I was taking some psychology courses. Some of the things that I was witnessing these people do under certain conditions and the tables were turned, I could liken to some of the teachings they were trying to teach me in psychology. In other words, I was able to now take reality and make the book apply to it . . .

C: Sure.

D: . . . rather than trying to apply the reality later on to the book after I did the training like a basic student or I wouldn't still be doing the job.

C: Sure.

D: That was a unique experience.

C: Yeah.

D: I was able to write various papers for psychology classes and base it on reality. I was able to take some of that trained animal stuff and relate it to a human person and write papers on it. I did real good with those papers . . .

C: I'll bet you did!

D: Needless to say.

C: Fascinating!

D: Uh . . . it was something different than what you would get in the norm.

C: Sure.

D: There were a couple of things that took place in my mind as this thing developed and one of them happened right after that club was supposedly thrown. Our institution was under a little renovation. That was part of our problem. They were able to get into gasoline and everything else. And there were some things that they did to us in the yard with gasoline and the scare tactics. But they had demolished a yard toilet area and they had built a wooden one opposite kitty-corner of the yard, right next to the entrance way to where they came out of. And of course, in the original there was locked cabinets where they put a lot of mops and brooms and everything else, you know, sticks, clubs. They keep those away from the inmates. Well here, because of the renovations, they were right out in the open.

C: Yeah.

D: Of course, as they got keys, they would have gotten them anyway. It didn't make much difference. But because they were sitting in this fabricated structure, they put some toilets for the yard toilet area, as they broke out of that doorway, I heard a lot of breaking and splintering and stuff. As I walked toward that edge of the door, here were these inmates busting up these broom handles and the clubs. Now, I tell you at that point in time I was not under my own control. I was being ushered into the yard permanently. And yet my instant appearance on the scene, they stopped dead in their tracks.

C: Is that so?

D: How we control through the psychology, of a few handling the many, you just didn't do those things because there were rules and regulations you were to be reported on. I mean we could report them. So with my presence all of a sudden, they stopped dead in their tracks. I sort of ran by them and as I broke away and couldn't see them, I could hear the breaking taking place again. They wouldn't break the rule with me watching them. And yet, I was a hostage at that time. Psychology.

C: Yeah.

D: The . . . the reaction of people.

C: Yeah.

D: The trained behavior patterns.

C: Patterns. Yeah.

D: Those patterns were there. But those patterns were breaking down when I wasn't there. Of course this is how this whole thing developed. It was giving a period of time for these people to develop these habit changes.

C: Uh huh.

D: Until a certain few took over. And I only stated that there was probably, when I was hostage, probably about 50 inmates of a total population of 1600 at that time that did this.

C: Really?

D: So the rest of the population was being herded. They actually herded inmates. The kitchen crews were herded up out in the corner. If they weren't part of that, they were herded off in certain places to be used for the certain few who were trying to get their points across. And part of that 50 were people we had locked up until they got released out into the yard. Then it settled in. It settled in. The scare tactics . . . they managed to get their hands on gasoline. They would throw gasoline. I had gasoline thrown on my clothes and not just thrown on my feet as a scare tactic. I guarantee . . . I was scared.

C: Yeah.

D: There was one point over there when I really got scared. I mean I really wondered, "If this is the end, am I going to die this way?" Uh . . . apparently they thought some of our, see we didn't have the CERT [Correctional Emergency Response Team] teams in those days with the orange uniforms. We had people that had maybe state grays and the fellows came up one of the outside yards and I guess they probably were the State Police. Of course the usual fool would start saying the State Police are coming. They are going to break in on us. They are going to start killing us. Well the hostages will be wasted. I remember somebody somewhere had gotten a fire axe. God knows where the hell they got a hold of one of the fire axes. And I remember they laid their fire axe on my shoulder and I was scared of dying because I didn't want to die with a fire axe. Shoot me or something, you know. But I don't, I don't want my head chopped off with a fire axe. They laid it on my shoulder. At that point in time I was rather unnerved. But that was the only real instant where it really got to me and it only happened for a few instances then it disappeared.

C: Yeah.

D: Well, all the time I wondered, "Where the hell did the fire axe go?" All the time looking for it, you know, "Where is it at? How far away is it from me?" That, that is the reaction that I had at that point in time.

C: Yeah. What goes through your mind when you're at the point when you think "I'm going to die?" What do you think about?

D: It's awful hard. Don't forget we're talking about, we're talking uh . . . 17 years ago. Going on 17 years ago, 16 this year to be exact.

C: Yes.

D: Uh . . . Attica was 15 years ago. And 16, 16–1/2, 15. That'd be about it. So consequently I don't know. I do know that I had enough presence of mind to remember certain things and to do little bitty things. Some things will stand out forever. But what am I going to do to help myself with one of those. Maybe my mind is occupied in how I am going to preserve myself. Regardless though, I don't want to die this way.

C: Yeah.

D: What am I going to do to stop it? Most of the stuff after that, there was one officer sitting next to me. And I don't know if he had broken down a little, I don't know why I thought maybe he needed some talking to. I whispered in his ear and I says, "If anything goes wrong, hit the ground and we'll back into the benches." The only protection we've got. I hope we don't get shot.

C: You were thinking of . . .

D: The benches. I was thinking of how I am going to preserve myself. Because nobody can help me.

C: Nobody.

D: Out of that thought process over a period of years, I became a maverick in my field because I thought to myself there is only one thing that can save a person in this type of situation—you, yourself, and your ability to keep your wits. You, yourself, to prevent it from happening through whatever it takes, never to have any breakdowns in psychology again. Those are going through my mind out there. Now being mixed in with whatever is going on in that period of five hours, I can't really evaluate to say that I was scared shitless here, so to speak.

C: Sure.

D: And I was . . . you sit here, and I was very rational here. I think it was a mixture of it all. That at any given moment, depending on just what happened, and things were happening . . .

C: Yeah.

D: Like you had to go from one phase to another. I think that is what kept me from, from really having a nervous breakdown at that time. Now don't get yourself wrong, after Attica, I probably came as close to a nervous breakdown as people want to come to. That was maybe over, maybe a different reaction type pattern.

C: Sure.

D: It was all over. In Auburn I was lucky. After all these thought processes took place I was, I had left the yard. I was one of the last ones to leave the yard, with the Lieutenant. I went up front. I was supposed to be interviewed by State Police and what not. I didn't. We had an institution to get back together again. I guess I felt at that point in time, or after that was over, that I must be a professional in my job. Cause some of the things I said, because I had worked in the kitchen area. Some of the things I had said and done they immediately asked me to go down and try and put some people together in the kitchen to feed 1600 people.

C: As you, the moment you came out?

D: Within a half-hour.

C: You went back to work?

D: I went back, grabbed the keys and right back down to work. Part of the kitchen areas, I was just released shortly before 3 o'clock. I just finally headed out of that institution at about 11:30 that night after I had tried to cut corn beef on slicers that were partially broken and corned beef doesn't cut too easy to make sandwiches. Then we had to hide everything because the crew had come through and were busting all the locks. We hid the stuff. They couldn't find it at 6 o'clock in the morning. Got me out of bed. Had to have all these sandwiches, ran back in to work. I had hidden it secretly. Now I was able to function just as normally, if not more normally because I turned on, I guess, to the emergency of the situation.

C: Yeah. Did . . .

D: I guess I thought that after that was over I must be a professional in my job.

C: Yeah.

D: Because I am. I am still with the State.

C: Still there . . .

D: And I still haven't broken down or yelling. I am an involved type person.

C: Yeah.

D: I stayed very active. So consequently I didn't even break down maybe like I should have. That was my own doing really at Attica because I reached that breakdown state after Attica was all over with.

C: Later . . .

D: I reached that point.

C: Yeah.

D: My wife and some other people witnessed that. Maybe that was my help also at that time because that one breakdown type thing. The day went rather quickly and I went back to Auburn and functioned like down in the, what I call the bowels of the institution. I went right back to my job structure and functioned.

C: Right back.

D: This was right after Auburn [riot] I had an area in the kitchen area where I would have upwards to 140 inmates around me at any one time and I would be alone. It was the kitchen, recreational basement area.

C: Okay.

D: I went back down to that area and I couldn't get relief officers so I ended up working 12 hour days because the institution was open that long because of our shutdown after that, which was administrative. Which I am not going to explain much what we did or why.

C: Okay.

D: There were long hours in there and I worked those long hours. I worked a lot of overtime after that. Never a breakdown. Never a chance for me to let it all out. You're looking for a reason for that, I'd like to have you tell me why I would function that way. Why I would be a glutton for, I'd like to, I'd like to come up with answers. I've come up with varying answers of . . . professionalism. I wanted to make a lot of money. I felt maybe I could straighten things out. I have certain ideas.

C: Hmm.

D: Prior to that. Those ideas had come full circle because of the conditions which I was in along with a lot of my friends. I never wanted them to happen again. I felt maybe I could change things.

C: Uh huh.

D: These are all mixed in together as to my motivation.

C: Lots of motivation.

D: Boy, I would say that there is a multiple causation effect as they taught me in Criminal Justice.

C: Yeah.

D: In the psychologies that there is definitely a multiple causation effect to anything. It isn't any one thing that will develop.

C: Right.

D: But a combination of various things and various ways will then effectively, you know, do things. Will effectively make people do things. You're the psychologist. So you're going to be saying to . . . you can take these patients and put this stuff together and come up with some answers.

C: Yeah. Yeah. What sort of feedback did you get from friends or family or associates, afterwards, in the days, weeks after . . .

D: All of the long hours I worked about the only contact I had with people was with my wife and my kids. The kids were young . . .

C: I see.

D: They had been scared shitless and my wife had been scared shitless. Excuse the language. They had been scared out of their wits. My wife was. Apparently somewhere in there one of our well-meaning chaplains managed to call the house about, my wife said somewheres between 12 and 1 the kids had been sent home. They were closing the schools in Auburn because of this . . .

C: I heard that.

D: . . . situation.

C: Was there like a city . . .

D: . . . panic? Just a little bit. The mayor and everything else at that time, the word coming up wasn't like it is today, controlling . . . (the information)

C: Right.

D: Just utter chaos.

C: So they were probably afraid of a break-out, or . . .

D: My kids had come home and they had riled my wife up because they were being let out because there was a massive prison break and guards were being killed and, you know. All this stuff went through their minds. And their father was in there I suppose. They're impressionable kids in a grade school, at the elementary school level. Shortly after they got home my wife received a call from the chaplain at the prison who just politely stated that "Your husband is held hostage in the institution. We don't know what condition he is in." Then he hung up. I have never forgiven the chaplain for that. I worked with him for many years by that time and never forgave him for that.

C: Right.

D: I never really approached the matter but I never forgave him. I never considered him a professional any more. I tolerate him because of his title and because of the structure he had. But as a man, as a person, never. Not to this day. He has since retired just a little while ago. He left Auburn approximately 2–3/4 years ago. That was the last I seen of the man. But in any event, my contact, contact with my family was difficult because of that. My wife was probably in worse shape than I was.

C: How did it affect her?

D: I never really knew until I went to Attica. She was at her hairdresser, I was on the roof fixing a roof when the Attica riot broke out. I got called to the phone. I was told to come to the prison immediately. There was trouble. I hopped on a motorcycle. I was one of the first officers to report to the facility. I went in to the prison. I was one of the first officers to leave and headed for Attica with a car load of five people, including a Lieutenant who had worked at Attica. Went back up there.

C: You were working at Attica?

D: No. I was working at Auburn.

C: Working in Auburn but got called to Attica.

D: There were four officers and this Lieutenant in this car. Five officers and this Lieutenant and this guy made six of us in a small car. I don't know, we were doing 90 all the way up to Attica. We got to Attica and I went in. And various things took place that first day in Attica and I remember about 6 o'clock at night calling home and talking to my wife on the phone. And I said, "Hon, I'm in Attica." Obviously by now everything is all over the papers and she asked me one question: "Why in hell are you there? Why you?" I will never forget those words. Because I couldn't answer them. "Why was I there?" I didn't have to go to Attica. I could have declined it. But I had been through a hostage-taking. Why did my mind do these things? It hurt my wife very badly. And it took a long time to mend that rift with my wife.

C: Yeah.

D: Even to the point where my marriage almost broke up. I guess I was job oriented, to a point where I lost sight of my family to some extent. Never really enough that would kind of erupt . . . there were a lot of psychological problems in there.

C: Yeah.

D: That is where I started to relax with family. I have a job. A job I can handle. The job I was professional at. The job I wasn't scared of. The job I could go back and get it all done. And I proved it. I proved it by my personal record. It was proved by the hours I put in. What I did after being held a hostage.

C: Afterwards.

D: And what I did after Attica. And why I stayed in Attica until the bottom line and the place was put back together and had some semblance of order. I stayed there for two solid weeks. I was one of the last officers to leave Attica. Boy, I have never been able to answer that. Why? Because I never answered to my wife. She since adjusted to that. We since straightened out our problems. We have been married for 30 years.

C: Great.

D: And we were probably as happily married now as we were the day we were married.

C: Good for you.

D: I will tell you. It was a rocky road in there.

C: Yeah.

D: I was job oriented. It was hostage oriented.

C: Mhmm.

D: If you're looking for things that hostage situations can do to people, oh yeah, it can ruin your family life. Can do tremendous things in that.

C: You have seen some of that?

D: I have been there.

C: Yeah.

D: I have been there. I don't have to talk from . . . I have been through this stuff.

C: Yeah.

D: So it wasn't so much the job, I mean, it was the family. Why didn't I talk to someone because the family is involved and I work so long on the job I was talking to my peers on the job.

C: Yeah.

D: Some of my peers felt it was best to go back in that basement area and work with those inmates. They wouldn't even relieve me. That is why some of the long hours started. I then got involved shortly thereafter with the disciplining. I sat with tape decks and we were just starting a new discipline system ordered by the courts or as an answer to the court problems. It was from 1968 and on when these institutions started to change. Part of the problems came from those changes within the institutional structure that we are looking into today. We went through those trials of changing the thinking and everything else. I have gone through them. Today I have a different outlook, definitely different outlook for my job.

C: Uh huh.

D: Different approach to my job. The professionalism hasn't changed. I have asked for answers to questions that are in my head that I think . . . uh . . . I would say that I never, ever really reacted. Today I take a chance of being taken hostage at any given moment. It doesn't bother me. I pretty much . . . I pretty much feel I will never be taken hostage through my own ability to control the environment around me. And that's where I became a maverick. I had ideas that I think that Administration, you say this up here, forget it. I got to live down there. We are going to do it this way. I may break the wall, stay the hell off my back. I am going to keep myself and my brother officers, we're going to keep ourselves from being taken again. They gave training sessions after that. We had the outreach from our [training] academy.The outfits of some of the training courses they sent, they used to send questionnaires down about what kind of training you think you should put in there. Umm . . . combat training. Oh, yes! But there was also some psychology stuff down there too. And my answers were all for the psychology. The ability to control, the ability to change, the ability to do this. Of course, I was outgoing. You know. The gung ho people were in charge. But over a period of time they decided let's go with the psychologists.

C: Hmm.

D: And one of the answers I had if I was asked I was going to say, "Well, I tell you something. I have been there. I will tell you right now, you can take all the batons in the world, all the guns in the world, you can take everything you have inside of the place and you're dead. The only thing that will protect you in that yard is a Sherman tank and your butt in it and hope that they don't have any gas that will fire you out of it." Because that is the only protection you got down there. Other than your own mind, your own head, and your own mouth. Start using it.

C: Yes.

D: Or learning how to use it. Today the Department is run that way.

C: Yeah. I see.

D: Well, what I said is back in 1970, 71, and into 72, now it's real life in the Department and Mr. ———— will tell you that. These are the courses they teach.

C: Yeah.

D: Your ability to control others through many things. Your culture, you are this, you are that.

C: Sure. You really spear-headed . . .

D: No, because I didn't effectively make change except around me. I didn't go to Albany. I was asked to, boy, all those years ago. And I used to tell, you know, you go and train them around and send them back to me and I will teach them what it is like and I will teach them how to do it right. My own area. I didn't impose on many people.

C: I see.

D: I, maybe, I missed something there. Maybe I'm remiss for that.

C: Uh huh.

D: But I did effectively make change around me and around people with me. The job structure for the Sergeant and the Lieutenant was effectively controlled for that type of an approach. I entered the Watertown Correctional Facility and they used the hard-headed max approach that they learned out of Auburn. I changed that. I got the unions and everybody else up to date. Today it is done that way. Today I have a very low caseload. I have a very low incidence of discipline. Not me alone, but the Superintendent, the Dep's, are all at the same look-alike. There are some hotheads and some "cops" down inside that I effectively control. You don't do it that way. Use a pen, use a lot of brains and use psychological control and mind is a better type of psychology. I am not a trained psychologist. Mine came from whatever I got out of the books . . .

C: Books . . .

D: . . . and whatever I lived with 30 years controlling people and people's minds. By moving with them.

C: It's, it's real life learning . . .

D: That's exactly what I do. I manipulate. That's exactly what I do. I manipulate.

C: Yeah.

D: So out of all I had, basically, I had all those years before the riot or they wouldn't have come up. They wouldn't have come up before the hostage situation. They were there. The hostage situation emphasized certain things that gave me the guts to stick up for my own protection.

C: Yes.

D: I got that out of it. And maybe that's why that fear syndrome never really entered into it. I was answering questions in the morning as to why I was here, what was I functioning in? How will I function in the future? What needs to be changed? Why did this happen?

C: Why.

D: Uh . . . what can I do to effectively change that? What kind of a fight am I going to have? And I had a lot of fights.

C: Yeah?

D: People around me that, we created over time quite a team around me. I took some, like, some uh . . . supervisors above me. I took them on and, some of them won't leave the old style. Well, they used the old style, but they did it my way. I effectively controlled it. I effectively knew what was going on through others. I have an advantage today. I don't use the rat system as it is in a correctional facility. I utilize the employee being made to give bits and pieces back that somebody can pull those reins, put those pieces together, and it was 99 percent correct. He's going to be running it based on feedback from professional people not on a rat trying to get him to believe what he should believe.

C: Hmm.

D: Sure you get bits and pieces out of rats and they are good but you cannot run an institution based that way.

C: Yeah, Mhmm.

D: I fought that for a long time. And yet I seem to know everything that was going on in the institution as well as the people that used the system. That's what kept me from going I suppose.

C: As if you were in charge.

D: Because I fought people over this.

C: Yeah.

D: These were convictions that I had. If a rat misleads me, good. I'm doing battle with a rat. If I have professionals mislead, I'm going to be 99 percent correct and therefore I will be a winner anyway, even though I am a little off base or wrong. I'm going to gain out of all that the reputation of being accurate, of being, this man knows what the hell's going on. Let's not bug him. Therefore, my style of psychology control then works.

C: Uh huh.

D: You're going to have to, I'm giving you the overall view of, I suppose, three-quarters of a lifetime career. You're going to have to get certain things that maybe you can bring out of me. On what I meant, have thought at a certain point in time. But this is the overall thing.

C: Yeah. I was wondering about that, like you say . . . the days after each of the riots, start with Auburn, you're working a lot. What, I don't want any names, but in terms of other hostages, other officers, what did you see as the after-effects? What did people talk about or what did it seem to do to people? What meaning did people give this?

D: The majority of the people that worked around me went back on the job with no trouble. We would talk about, we talked very little about it really. We would talk more about what are we going to do in the future.

C: Uh huh.

D: Don't forget a lot of people that were taken with me were taken out of the kitchen area, officers that I worked with day in and day out.

C: Yeah.

D: It was in the same and some of those people were supervisors and they are still officers or have retired.

C: Yeah.

D: I don't know why. Maybe because we didn't want to talk about it. That part of it.

C: Hmm.

D: But maybe some of those people were in the same ball game as I was . . . see anybody that was down in there was, there was no supervisors down there. There was one Lieutenant that sat down with us who never really liked the Administration for what took place to him. He was the only supervisor that was with us. We were all officers, so who would have related to us to that but a fellow officer.

C: Sure.

D: Ah . . . this one Lieutenant didn't come back to work for a little while and they, they hit him in the back side and messed his kidneys up trying to get the gates opened up and the officers wouldn't open it up for him naturally. You know, there are certain things that we just wouldn't do. We had been trained not to do.

C: Uh huh.

D: The officer at the gate, "I'm sorry man, I ain't opening this gate." They would punch him again in the kidneys. And as to why he was there and some of the things that were said afterwards, about the, I will never forgive some of them, some of the Administrators. So the people I related with would have been strictly the officers that I worked with.

C: Uh huh.

D: So we are going to be more relating on a work basis. With an occasional reference to the hostage circle, but on a more or less of an overall basis, not on a personal basis.

C: Oh, yeah.

D: "Hey, man, did you shit your pants out there on the bench?" Or, you know, things of that nature.

C: Yeah.

D: I don't know what the thought patterns were. You've interviewed ——— —— who sat there and was taken out of the kitchen.

C: I did.

D: You've interviewed ———, who was taken as an officer out of the control center outside the kitchen area.

C: Yes.

D: And they did an awful job on him because he was what they call checkpoint Charlie. He was a very tough individual.

C: Uh huh.

D: All of us were to some extent, but he seemed to stand out as the most. And they really tried to work his mind over out there.

C: Really targeted him out.

D: Treated, and I felt very sorry for him because he had been able to become very visible.

C: Yeah. He was a real target.

D: He was a target. I wasn't so much a target. I was just one of those that was out there. I do remember at one point that someone coming from the kitchen walked up behind me, somehow he got close to the hostage circle, and he says, "Hey Captain, don't worry, we're going to watch out for you." And "You don't deserve to be here" and things of that nature. Then he walked away. I don't know even if maybe that reassured me that we weren't really alone down there. But, control wise, these people were in as bad shape as we were.

C: Yeah.

D: They were subject to anything that might take place any time. There was only a few that were governing many.

C: Yeah.

D: The 50 inmates that had taken us over were really taking the place of the 50 officers that normally run the place.

C: Yeah.

D: It psychologically transitioned, that's exactly what took place.

C: Yeah.

D: And we allowed that to happen through various things, myself included because I was down inside.

C: Uh huh.

D: And why I say after it was all over with, I'd never allow that after what they told me. I would never allow these conditions to happen. I would act on my own. To hell with anybody that disobeyed an order. If I was right I wouldn't be taken hostage and therefore, I would be doubly right and I would handle any kind of a problem with my supervisor. If we ever reached those conditions again. Going in to Attica and watching what happened there, and how it kept going on for four days, totally convinced in my mind that I had been right. And that observation.

C: Yeah.

D: What I have been in my career . . . I've been . . . I've been able to control my own destiny.

C: Hmm.

D: I guess I wanted to control it. And if I could help others at the same time—fellow officers—then they would ride that crest with me. You know, make it work.

C: Yeah.

D: And I have. I have been able to control, basically, psychologically I can control the whole institution from this psychological, through the discipline system. And it is working.

C: Working.

D: Works better than in most institutions. I just got through talking to the Lieutenant at Midstate. They called about something. I says well "Why did you get that problem?" I says, "I stamped that problem out two and one-half years ago." I says, "What are you doing wrong down there?" So, other institutions are medium just like we are. In fact there is a Lieutenant that runs, that used to be in Watertown. He was the one that started the system in Watertown.

C: Really!

D: And they took it over after a couple of lieutenants worked for half a year, I came into Watertown and took it over.

C: I see.

D: So consequently, I executioned out those problems that I don't got. So maybe my system is working. The trouble with this type of business is you *never* know until it is all over if it works or not.

C: If it works.

D: It's not too happy. Say you're trying to come up with the rhyme and reason to make it work. First, you learn about the results afterwards because then the results are going to be right.

C: Yeah.

D: It is a good administrative approach and I think it is working. But it takes the people in between to make it work. And ain't going to do it from the Central Office saying this is the way you should do it.

C: No. You need the people.

D: You've got to believe in that. Directives, laws, are not going to make that.

C: No.

D: Not going to make that overall change for control.

C: No. You need the human beings too.

D: Individually, you keep people in line for control. Out of this, I suppose the development of what I got out of this was the motive to do my job. I feel better. My ability to control destinies, control people and manipulate and any other word you want. I got the training in the hostage situation in Auburn and looking at it in Attica because we can't go to this. We can't have those people getting hurt, choked and other chaos it brings afterwards.

C: So, you're really talking about some beneficial effects from that experience.

D: I definitely believe that that experience was beneficial to me.

C: You do?

D: Take it by the minor psychologies of my own of being truthful, or having problems with my family structure. I think that I'm better because of it.

C: Uh huh.

D: I wouldn't advise anybody to go through a hostage situation to learn or to get that experience.

C: Yeah. Right.

D: It's. That's not healthy. But I haven't lost for it. I think I gained for it.

C: Gained something.

D: I gained tremendously from it.

C: How about that.

D: It's hard to say what, well, what would I be like today if I hadn't been held hostage in Auburn or if I hadn't been involved in what happened at Attica? It would . . . it is impossible to answer that.

C: Sure.

D: I am what I am today and I do feel that some change was made because of that. I don't know where I would be without it.

C: Just . . .

D: I might be better without it. Who will ever know. History is made each minute as you spend your life.

C: That's right. You said that Attica seemed to have affected you more profoundly than Auburn did.

D: Yeah.

C: Can you talk about that a little bit?

D: I always wondered why and the only answer I can ever come up with in my mind is because in Auburn I had control. I was aware of control to be taken care of on the spot. Like I said, you can't control it from the front of the ivory tower. It's got to be controlled right there like you and I are sitting straight on to each other. We're controlling something at this point nobody out there in that living room is able to have a hand in it.

C: Yeah.

D: And if there was a Dep sitting out there and I was talking to you he would try to influence me because he has the authoritive control, in an institutional setting, that is basically the way it works. So consequently, I was able to sit inside and sort of control that. At Attica I sat outside and had no control. I reacted more to Attica not being able to do anything. Not being able to. It's my ego, I suppose, I'm a little bit of that.

C: Your helplessness.

D: My helplessness. My feelings that if I were down inside and if we were inside, we could handle this situation. I can't handle it from up here. So I was having frustration. I was having frustration because I saw superiors do things in Attica that I didn't agree with. I saw mistakes being made that I didn't agree with. There was no wandering any deeper into that because we still have problems from some civil litigations in Attica. I'm still subject to go in to court for those. The criminal stuff was over with. I was still going to court in Buffalo five years after that when they finally gave amnesty except for the person that actually killed Quinn, the C.O. Total amnesty was granted throughout the State to the troopers, anybody that fired a shot, anybody that, you know, inmates. Everybody but the killer of Quinn. Total amnesty was granted. Our court, that was done by our Governor. That was about five and one-half years after. It was probably in 1976, somewhere along there. I was still driving back and forth to Buffalo everyday to appear in court. I tore a car up doing that for a period of about three or four years.

C: Hmm.

D: On this second go around of trials for that stuff. But there still is civil litigation. There is still things I will never disclose about Attica. I do disagree with them in the report. I know why it was written and basically it worked. You see the State got the right to run into the institutions to try to bring itself up out of the chaos. I don't agree with what was in that book because 90 percent of it was the untruths, half truths, or maneuverings to half certainties. And maybe 20 years down the road when everything is all over with I might, I might give you some idea what I mean by that. [Laughter] The only thing I will go into [about] Attica are some personal observations and some of the feelings that maybe I went through and that is basically what you want.

C: Right.

D: The frustration of having to stand up there and wait. Waiting on everybody. Not just me. The fact that it went as long as it did meant that there was no way they could ever control, take over of that institution. I used gas. I was one of the humane ones. I refused side arms. I refused firearms. Put it that way. I utilized gas that day. I had a gas gun. Gas cartridge and everything else. I was deployed with the State Police.

C: You mean that they . . .

D: They were with the takeover. They were the takeover. Frustration right up to that point. Nothing I could do. Nothing anybody else could do. There were people on the roofs with guns that didn't belong up there with guns. They weren't trained. We didn't have the CERT Teams in those days, etc. We had State Police in there and you had better believe that people recognize people. I did it myself. I recognized faces that had held me hostage in Auburn. If I had been armed with a firearm I could have evened the scale of justice. Thank God I didn't carry one. Thank God my conviction was not the use of firearms. My conviction was to try and use the pop gases, the mind. Beat a person down using the pin, my mouth and just take them apart psychologically, I suppose. That has always been my background. Apparently . . .

C: Right.

D: I had it at Attica, of course.

C: Yeah.

D: I was offered a side arm. I was told I had to carry it because I had to protect the gas equipment. My reply to that was, "That side arm is useless to me." That gas gun can't blow me away. That gun could be taken away from me and somebody could blow me away five times. They can't get this gas gun away from me. And if they do, they are going to have a hell of a time trying to fire it. I mean if I'm going to be able to get out of harm's way, forget your side arms. It is useless to you. I haven't got a hand free to handle it. Keep it. Well I was told that you know. There is chaos in there. You didn't obey orders. So that is what the breakdown was in Attica. There was just too much going on. There was no way any one person including the Governor could ever control that.

C: Uh huh.

D: My frustration kept building and building until finally we went in. Everybody did their thing. Me included. I didn't do it, the gut feeling thing, because I had only gas and it was the humane way. And that proved out in front of the McKay Commission when I was taken in front of them. Also proved out in front of the Grand Jury, which I won't explain. The frustration of the final day when we went in. Things that I saw bothered me very much. I went in with the first wave. Way behind the first wave was the, the second wave was the support people which was gas, and backup and I was in the second wave but I was probably within 20 feet of the men using the scale ladders, get in the yards quick to get to the hostages. I do remember I had some grave misgivings about the safety of the hostages. Knowing Auburn's set up, knowing what went through my mind in Auburn, "How will I save myself?" knowing that those people's minds out there usually were all fucked up and they couldn't think for themselves. By this point in time I was totally convinced of that. That there would be no way that they could save themselves. There would be *no* way under what we were told in Auburn and some of the same people were doing it regardless of what the preparations are. There was *no* way that those people in that yard could, there was no way we could get to them. I don't give a damn what we did fast enough. History proved I was right. God forbid, but I guess this proved I was right. People were killed out there. Maybe not by inmates but by the over-rashness to get in to those people. There were hostages killed. The whole operation. I took part in it. I was trained to take part in. I took part in it because I am involved. I took part in it because I have certain convictions to try and do whatever I could. The frustration of being out and not in. I had to get in there. But in the back of my mind, I thought this wasn't going to work. There is just no way, in my experiences in Auburn in that short-lived five hours that I had under those conditions. But this is never going to come out right.

C: Apprehensive.

D: It has been too long. I've watched ditches being dug. I've watched bunkers being built. I mean it was unbelievable the power of people's minds that would spend some time. They actually thought, those inmates actually thought that they were invincible. How are you going to handle something of that nature? You have martyrs that have built themselves and they have waited there for four long days and let them do it.

C: Let it build up.

D: One of the things I said after I called my wife, I went right back down on the job until we got relieved at 9 o'clock, 10 o'clock that night. I caught a few hours sleep. Went back in. We were on 12 and 12 at that point. I was always there during the day time. But I remember going back down inside and I kept saying why doesn't anybody ever listen to me. I am just some officer who didn't know anything. They didn't. Why didn't they go in? They can't let it go over. If they let it go overnight, let it go overnight, and people are going to die. They let it go over night and these people still feel they are still invincible, you aren't going to talk them out of nothing! You don't work with a black man by allowing him to build himself up because he becomes invincible. That is the ego maniac, egotism that a black type personality has.

C: Yeah.

D: He can build himself up to Muhammad Ali and other God-type things. The next morning they had owned Attica and thought that they owned the world. And subsequent days after that, things they did, things that we observed, things we observed on the day of the takeover, proved that I was right. That's history. That is part of the takeover. Nothing I'm disclosing there isn't written.

C: Right.

D: Then, at the time of the going in, and the taking over of the, of the institution, in back of the institution, that first wave went roaring through, I was in the second wave. I suppose this is the closest combat I'll ever see in my lifetime. What had taken place? I mean, it was combat when I went in, right? I am not a combat man. I was in the military police; I was in the service. I was never in combat attire. Yet I went in that way. What I witnessed as I went in; death, destruction, people withering and dying in front of me.

C: Hmm.

D: And that is when my mind started to react to it. I functioned. I functioned very well that day. I didn't use brutality. There was brutality going on all around me. There were inmates in there that I had known in Auburn, knew they couldn't be any part of this riot. There were a lot of factions in there; at that time the inmates wore gray. There a gray meant guilty. Three men, I was recognizing faces I knew couldn't take part in this and I was attempting to try and get closer. Everybody was naked out there. They had men that were cripples. I tried to help these people. Believe it or not I tried to with, the State Police would hold in on them, and I would wander around, and this is after the takeover within an hour after the takeover, and I had gotten through the chaos, down in the yards wandering around. That's where I left off. I know I did things for about an hour and then all of the sudden my next recollection is the fact that I'm wandering around down there and I'm seeing State Police pushing people into action. I knew they were yelling out, hey that man's a cripple, there's no way he can take part in this thing. Back off. And I remember yelling at State Policemen. Deputy Sheriffs. I remember yelling at National Guardsmen. Back off. You had all these animals coming out of his shell besides the inmates themselves. I mean Attica belonged to us at that point in time. All the destruction was done. There were, there were these people and I tried to stop that. I tried to get involved. I tried to help. But I remember standing at the head of a block. The next thing I know I am out some more doors. The next thing I know I am standing at the head of what they call A Block bringing people back in. Running the gauntlet. That's where the name the gauntlet came from. And I am watching naked men run up through there and I am watching Deputy Sheriffs upending them with clubs. You know! I had an axe handle in my hand. I could kill 500 inmates I suppose. But the only thing I did on accident I tapped someone on the rear end and told them to hurry up before they get it, hurry up, move. And I was splitting them up. Some that way, some this way and we were trying to put them in four or five blocks. But I witnessed all of that stuff. And I know that at one point that years later with the union lawyers and in front of the grand jury I wanted to tell them what I saw. I could not rat on another law enforcement agency.

C: Yeah.

D: I saw things happen there. I never said this until the criminal stuff was all over with. I didn't like some of the things I saw. Most of the officers in there were under total control because we still had it. Most of the State Police were under control while they were still there because they had their own supervisory staff. We had our supervisory staff. The National Guard was okay because they did have supervisory staff. There were Deputy Sheriffs in there. I remember looking close at the shields. I will never forget the words written on those shields. Those people had no supervisor.

C: Yeah.

D: They were not trained.

C: Yeah.

D: To me a Deputy in those days weren't trained like they are today even.

C: Yeah.

D: And those Deputies some of them were brutal. A lot of what you will hear out of Attica about the brutality after the riot. It wasn't done by the Corrections Department. It wasn't done by the State Police and it wasn't done by the National Guard either. You can draw your own conclusions. Because I will never accuse anybody. I was sworn to secrecy by our union lawyers. And I wanted to and I tell you I wanted to . . .

C: Yeah. You were angry.

D: I was, maybe my, my frustration with that. This was years later. After this was all over with I stayed in there and tried to put some order in the place and of course I stayed for an additional ten days, and went back. In the meantime, the Attica things had been announced well over the radio. My wife knew where I was at. She knew my involvement. She was concerned. She came up with another officer's wife. They drove up together. My wife knew some people so she managed to get herself down inside. I mean down on the State Road. She knew ———. She said the right words, got through the roadblock and got up inside. A lot of people couldn't get through. This other woman wouldn't have gotten through but I knew ———. I worked with ———.

C: Yeah.

D: He was the Deputy Superintendent. So consequently she managed to get to the State Housing that he was in and then walked back down in front of the prison. They wouldn't let them on the property. They let them off the State Road, a few people. Because she had the right names and she had to walk on the opposite street. She stayed in a small dime store, small corner store kind of thing right across from the entrance way to Attica. I had no idea she was there. The other officer that I was involved with from Auburn who was ——— —. He came back and he had gone outside and came back in and he said our wives are out front. He said out front. "They're out front?" "Yes, they're out front." I didn't say too much. I said okay and this is probably around 2 o'clock in the afternoon. About 2 o'clock in the afternoon, somewhere around there. Within an hour or two I got myself where I went out front. I walked out the main gate at Attica. I saw her across the street. I started across that parking lot. I got pretty much to the road. But she didn't dare come. About as I got to the road, she broke from the other side of the road. We met in the middle of the street. I went down on my knees and I cried like a baby. Well that's the closest I think I ever want to come to another breakdown. That's the only time in my life I ever felt that way. Now maybe that was the combination of Auburn, total frustrations, people that don't want to take the proper training that think they can beat their way out of a band box with a club with a thousand people keeping them in there. Other than Attica itself were frustrations that I didn't want to come out on that road that day, that afternoon. But you know something, I got relieved, I went back inside. Finished up. I was able to function. Went back out, went home. And back up the next morning went back to work at Attica at the State Prison. Now why? Why did I have that much strength in me? I will never know. These are the answers I will never have. Maybe you, you might accomplish . . . [Laughter] but that's what you're looking for is these human emotions.

C: Yeah.

D: At that point the total destruction within the prison system, the total indifferences to a lot of things was basically over. We started to build our institution. That is why I said the McKay Commission report did suffice. It wasn't good but it did do the job. Maybe I would have done the same thing if I was faced with certain responsibilities to put a system back in. We have been functioning ever since. We are now probably the best prison in the State of New York or [even] in the world. We are probably the most advanced; we probably have the best training techniques. I hate to say the death and destruction brought that but I have a feeling that what we are is because of Attica. I think we can set the standard for the country. We do set the standard in a lot of things for other countries. Our tier system, our system of discipline inside with the safeguard of the inmates' rights. And yet we can still function; we can still control.

C: Yeah.

D: We have total discipline and control and our system has all been studied by Canada. It is being studied by every state in the union.

C: Yes.

D: The American Correction Association which does uh . . . accreditations and we are accredited up here, find a lot of fault with our system because it isn't theirs. They actually tried to tear it down.

C: Really!

D: They can't touch it because it is governed by law. It's mandated by Supreme Court decisions that have come in from Miranda on up to these prisons day to day. I thank Albany for Legal Issues Training, I and II. I know and I have on my desk the full background of why we were doing what we are doing in this State. Why I believe in it. Plus what's in my head. Other Lieutenants will come down and take these books and go read them. I point out certain things that they should pick out of them besides all these Supreme Court decisions. The high points. I was taught very well in Albany by members of the State University System of Law.

C: Uh huh.

D: Fred Callahan. I think he is probably one of the best men I have ever listened to.

C: Yeah.

D: Probably one of the most astute people ever I listened to. He doesn't talk like they did many years ago from an outside viewpoint. He went inside and learned and then applied it that way. I probably would follow him to the ends of the earth.

C: That's crucial.

D: Uh . . . so I picked up a lot of what he said. And I brought a lot back. And I probably could teach others very well. That's about it. I have already done.

C: Okay.

D: I will influence people around me wherever I go. I will make up certain standards. I'm my own man, so-to-speak within the guidelines of the department, and definitely within the law and the right to speak. I don't need a gun.

C: Hmm.

D: In fact one of the adages I have had all along ever since I read it, "Gentlemen, you keep your guns out here, I'm going inside I'll put it down my way. If I hit the ground, then you can grab my gun and get my ass the hell out of there." Maybe that is why I went back to work. Maybe I feel like effecting change.

C: Yeah.

D: My background, my personnel records. Not just my lip service here. My personnel record, other people, to some respect, the ones that are, you know, a good influence.

C: Yeah.

D: My old records and everything else stand behind me.

C: Uh huh.

D: I suppose.

C: Reaction oriented.

D: With that adage . . .

C: You've seen a lot of officers at Auburn, at Attica, maybe Sing-Sing, or other incidents and you've probably seen a lot of variety, a lot of difference in the way people react to it immediately as well as over time. Can you, do you, have any hunches about how to account for those differences?

D: Just to keep them in mind. Everybody sees different. If we were all alike, what a hell of a world we would have.

C: Yeah.

D: Would we have an ideal state or not? No, everybody has their own thought process. Everybody has their own souls and their own minds.

C: Yeah.

D: Everybody has their own interpretations out of life. It is called personalities, too.

C: Yep.

D: I never try to figure out somebody's personality. I know it is there.

Sometimes it is anti to goals.

C: Mhmm.

D: I don't try to change a personality. I try to change the educational level.

C: Yeah.

D: I try to change the input and let THEM change their own personality. I can't change it for them.

C: Yeah.

D: I can't change their interpretation of things. I can expose them maybe. That's where the teaching comes in. I can stand in front of a classroom and talk to a hundred people. I would influence one of them. I can stand outside the institution and over a period of a couple of months probably influence a dozen people around me.

C: I see.

D: That's, that's my feelings.

C: Influence by action and by model and by example.

D: Now I've shown you.

C: Yeah.

D: And this is why it works, this type of thing rather than stand up and get it out of a book. Maybe it is because in my, in my years of schooling and my, I have a Degree in Correction Administration and I am about 20 hours away from a full-time four-year degree if I ever . . . I stopped doing it eight, ten years ago.

C: Uh huh.

D: But I am only 20 hours away from a full four-year degree in Professional Services.

C: Uh huh.

D: At Utica-Rome I was doing that in an off-campus type thing. So I do have a Degree in Correction Administration which I majored in the psychology. I effectively feel that what I got out of the book was only because of what I experienced.

C: Yeah.

D: And I as a teacher would then lose the effectiveness I had on the job by trying to teach it and become just another teacher out of a book.

C: Yeah.

D: I didn't want that. I guess that is why I never bothered to teach out of a book. My wife says I should. I could retire as a teacher and be a hell of a lot more than I am today. But you know something, I wouldn't be happy.

C: Hmm.

D: I am happy doing . . .

C: You like your job?

D: I like it enough to stay at it I suppose. I guess. I could retire almost six years ago. I'm staying at it. I will stay at it until I get tired of what I am doing.

C: Yeah.

D: But right now running the discipline in ———. That's my baby. I got good, I got good records. I've got, it shows that whatever I am doing is working.

C: A real sense of pride in it.

D: I got, I've got good feedback from the Superintendent from Albany. I stopped problems inside this institution that are still evident in other institutions. So that pride will keep me there forever.

C: Yeah.

D: I haven't any urge to go back to Auburn because I couldn't be effective in Auburn. I would be buried on nights for a long time. A larger institution, low on the seniority pole and all that jazz.

C: I see.

D: And I don't want to go back to those.

C: So you would rather be in an institution where you can have an impact?

D: I guess maybe that's my ego again. Now the only thing I can say is the background and other people will tell me if it is working or not.

C: Yeah.

D: My ego. But my ego is being satisfied.

C: What thoughts go through your mind when you hear about hostage-takings, say at Sing-Sing, say even Iran or Lebanon or . . . do you feel any particular . . .

D: Well, well there is a vast difference between being taken hostage in this country even in the prison system as versus a foreign country.

C: Right.

D: There, there is a definite difference. Here it is, I can relate to somebody in a prison setting or a . . . well, there's two things in this country we'll say. There is a prison setting which I am familiar with and then there is the nut that just grabs somebody trying to get out of something. And it is like a one-on-one.

C: Yeah.

D: Or one-on-two type situation. As where prison settings are usually 50-on-50 type thing and in mass. The prison setting isn't as dangerous really. Maybe you got, because you got people that are trained and can expect this at any time. The thought patterns are more of a, of a, like everybody around that hostage circle, I think one of the things in my mind now that you ask that question was, "I hope none of these guys goes off and causes, I hope none of these guys, you know, goes berserk on us."

C: Yeah.

D: Any of these officers. I am looking at eyes and faces across me to see. And of course nobody was. Everybody was professional enough to stay put and not cause trouble and get blamed. Our training allows us to do that calmly.

C: Stayed quiet. Yes. That helps.

D: The same thing happened in Attica. Nobody really went off on a berserk pattern and did anything like that. Same thing in Sing-Sing. Right. You can't expect that in a setting of grabbing a couple of girls hostage in a bank and trying to hold them.

C: Right.

D: You know. Somebody is liable to go berserk at any moment.

C: Right.

D: And all hell is going to break loose because they forced the issue.

C: They are not professionals.

D: Not professionals.

C: Yeah.

D: So there is a vast difference between that when I hear about a hostage being taken I don't think of it the same way, in a bank setting, or a corner store setting or just grabbing a cop, for that matter. Even a cop in that type of a setting. It is different than the setting we would have. Maybe it is because of the guns. You see in Attica they didn't have guns. Sing-Sing they didn't have guns. In Auburn they didn't have guns. They had other types of weapons.

C: Yeah.

D: Whereas the hostage-taking on the street invariably involves a firearm which is instantaneous death.

C: Right.

D: And by the same token I'd rather have a gun shot at me than a fire axe laid at my shoulder or swung at me. So mixed emotions right in there. Now we go out of this country and into some place like a foreign country where you hear of a hostage being taken, you cannot fathom. I know in my mind you can't, fathom exactly what those people are going to do because it is a, it isn't sane. It is a forever type situation.

C: Yeah. You think of it as a . . .

D: Here in this country it is a momentary-type thing.

C: Uh huh.

D: You know something has to happen sooner or later, very shortly. Over there, they take them and hold them for years. Now what could they have done to those people?

C: Yeah. No control.

D: How are those people reacting to that type of incarcerations?

C: Yeah.

D: Now the thought processes would be entirely different.

C: Yeah.

D: I don't think that much about it overseas. I am going to say, to hell, they shouldn't be over there in the first place. So I guess I blame them more or less because they were taken hostage.

C: Yeah. Yeah.

D: In my mind.

C: Yeah.

D: Maybe if their minds are screwed up, they asked for that. But by the same token, so did I when I worked inside a prison. I accepted the conditions and was willing to work in them. So do the women that work in these places too.

C: Hmm.

D: That's one of the other worries.

C: Sure.

D: They grab women and that's when they cause forward type reactions from the old syndrome that would affect the women and could upset a situation.

C: Yeah.

D: Like the Dallas situation.

C: Yeah. Sure.

D: In most hostage-takings based on what I've experienced from both sides of the fence, it is a very delicate situation. It takes fast, concise stuff to handle that. Today they are addressing it with intervention tools. You undoubtedly have explored those.

C: Somewhat.

D: They are a common thing in training. The next question might be, "Why don't I belong on a hostage intervention team?" I don't. I've been there. I'd be useless. My thought patterns would be useless today because I would revert automatically to myself and the situation and I can't do that.

C: You would identify with the ones . . .

D: Hostage intervention cannot have those, those emotions.

C: Need to keep it cool.

D: Because you will make mistakes. Because that is the training that they know. Hostage intervention buys the amount of time necessary but never buys more time like Attica and the resultant death.

C: Yeah.

D: I believe in the hostage intervention. I believe in some of the people putting on some of the teachings they've got.

C: They are on the right track.

D: After our riot, they asked me questions about it. They sent out questionnaires and stuff. It wasn't a personal thing. It was an impersonal piece of paper. It said, "Did you want to sit there while we negotiated? Would you want us to come in and get you?" My answer invariably, "Would you get your ass in here and get me!" Like I said, "I go down there and I will do my thing. But the instant I go down, you crash in there and get me out."

C: Fast!

D: Don't allow them to have the model that they think they can kill the world to get all the dead men.

C: Don't wait around.

D: You see, you got that psychological control. That little thing I saw breaking the broom handles coming out.

C: Yeah.

D: You got that instantaneous control for that split second.

C: You got it.

D: Use it.

C: Get in while you can.

D: Then get your ass the hell out of there. Get him. Attica didn't do that. They waited. Look at Attica.

C: They lost it. Yeah.

D: Auburn, they, they really didn't. What they did in Auburn is they, — —— was involved, he tried a different tactic. And they released them. It was a stand-firm tactic and it released them. I watched. But he is gone now. I watched Oswald do just the opposite. Very disagreeable to me. You better believe it. Those are my people down there. And they were being afforded the same thing I would want to be afforded if I was in their place. They asked me how to relate to a few of them. You see, you are bringing out bits and pieces by asking questions.

C: Uh huh.

D: Things that I would roll over in my mind.

C: Yeah.

D: Uh . . . in my mind was, they are leaving them down there. You've killed 'em. Go in and get them now. At least some of them got a chance. I would want that chance.

C: Yeah.

D: Come in and get me. I will take my chances of going over intervention and save my ass before they are organized. You let them get organized and I'm a dead man.

C: Yeah.

D: That's what happened in Attica. That's what didn't happen at Auburn. But I had been thinking in the back of my mind, "What am I going to do now? What am I going to do if they come in?" They got to come in. Through my mind was, "They got to come in and get us out of here. Now what am I going to do? Do I hit the ground and roll over to this bench? And hope for the best."

C: Yeah.

D: I can't fight. I can't fight. I remember telling that to the officer next to me. Hit the ground and let's get back on this bench together.

C: Hit the ground and roll.

D: They can't get us both. I think somewhere along that officer . . . there was something like that you know. I think he was starting to break and I was back, maybe that is why I went into these other people. And these people were, breaking, bring this favor down on us. Well, if there is something we can do, don't break. Just, just bear with it. Have the patience to bear with it. I know both those went through my mind and I did express them to the guy next to me. You know. Those are certain things that are, are what you call, certain type.

C: So, as you think about it, as I listen to you, certain moments are vivid as if they happened yesterday and other things are blacked out.

D: Like blacked out. I, I sort of call them the high waves, the things as to why I think today. Maybe that is why. Now I could completely change if I thought of other things. You know.

C: Yeah. If you were talking to say a small group of people who are going to serve as, as advisors of counselors in a post-hostage-taking situation for hostages, families and so forth and they were asking you the question, "What should we do to provide help or support for hostages and their families after the incident?"

D: Oh, after the incident? Oh, I was going to say. Okay. [Pause] Boy . . . see I helped myself so it is awfully hard for me to, because there was nobody to help me. Nobody. Nobody in God's earth ever came forward and tried to help me after being held hostage or helped me after going through Attica. *Nobody.* Nobody has ever come forward and said one word to me about, "What can we do to help you because of the trauma you went through?" The Department had no cares at that point. For one thing, they were very unfamiliar. Today maybe it is different. Maybe they do have this follow-up for people that were from Attica. Maybe they had it for some of the people at Attica that I wouldn't have been exposed to because I was an outsider, so to speak.

C: Right.

D: But I will tell you right now they sure as hell did not have it at Auburn.

C: Yeah.

D: Uh . . . they didn't even have a way of knowing of who all the hostages were. One of the things that I said I was very upset with was that when I came up front, when I left that yard, this is a good psychological thing. When I left that yard, I was the last one to leave with this Lieutenant. Why would, why stay behind and be the last one to leave? I remember someone in there almost volunteered to be the last one to leave the yard with the Lieutenant. Because they weren't going to let the Lieutenant go until the last one. I remember getting up with the Lieutenant and I remember starting to walk to the front. We got to the corner of the block. The keys were so screwed up. Everything was so screwed up down there, it was pathetic. And apparently couldn't do something. They thought the Lieutenant because of his rank would have it. He was an 11-7 Lieutenant who was supposed to be back in Elmira. Apparently he had gone and come back over. However, he had come back down in the yard to help out a little because he was the extra Lieutenant, or whatever it was. He ended up in the yard. I remember getting to the corner of the building. It was a new gym they were building there and they separated us. And they says, "Lieutenant we want you here." I says, "No he is going with me or I'm going with him." I remember a club coming down in front of me and says, "No, you're going to the front. He's going that way." And away I went. When I got to the gate it was one of those, "I could kiss the biggest officer I could find" type thing. I got up front and walked by the Superintendent's Office, supposedly for a debriefing. Maybe that's why I went back down inside because I was so disgusted up front. Went by the office and I guess I, they said, "———, get in here." And I came in. They said something about the hostages in the yard. I said, "There is nobody left in the yard but a Lieutenant." They said, "Oh, that's Lieutenant ———." I says, "No. That is Lieutenant ———." "Oh he's not down there. He is home in Elmira." I remember the reply I gave the Superintendent. I says, "You're full of shit." I says, "I just left the man. He *is* down there. Don't you people even know who the hell is in that yard?" I remember those remarks. I remember that, that, that, that, instant I wanted to smash him in the face. The Superintendent! What the hell the good are they? Don't tell me I'm wrong! I know who is down there, you weren't. They kept adamant that that man was not down there and he had been held hostage all day. And they had beat him in the kidneys. A lot of people had those . . . why, the ivory tower again.

C: Yeah.

D: Maybe I had a keen dislike for that administrative staff at that point.

C: Yeah.

D: But I was down back inside because of it. I wanted no part of this. Forget this. People wonder why we went back to work. Maybe that is what did it. I will never know what drove me back in that place. A lot of things. That multiple causation thing. Some of these things are, they didn't know who the hell was held hostage in that yard. Now, do something for us afterwards? They couldn't do anything for us while we were there because.

C: Yeah.

D: So. Utter chaos. They weren't trained in this stuff. This was the first time it happened in the State of New York since 1929 which is a lot of the people involved wouldn't remember that. My father might as a kid, you know. Nothing that would remember by the age group now that is working in these institutions. So I did whitewash that with the fact that everybody was in the same chaotic shape that I was. And yet, today I know what is expected of me with the rank I have. I know what I have to deliver. I know the mistakes I will not make at the expense of others and now I think they were totally wrong in those days. Even worse now I think after I look back.

C: You're more convinced.

D: But they didn't have half the names right that were hostages in that yard and I reacted to that but then I left and decided to go back to work. To wipe that out of my mind, that other frustration of, what the hell is this? I knew it was other frustrations as people had allowed the thing to happen.

C: Yeah.

D: And I will never disclose that because, you know those were decisions that were made. But the psychologies of reacting to the people up front . . .

C: Yeah.

D: They're . . . what would I, what would I say should be done for the people afterwards? [pff, whistle] I'm not going to rush up and say, that would be speculation on my part so like I don't think I had any thought processes about how to be helped.

C: Yeah.

D: Other than the fact that from that point on I developed, I'm going to help myself.

C: Did it yourself.

D: Nobody can help me. And not only be . . .

C: Do you . . .

D: Not only in the job approach but the psychologies and the hostages. My thoughts were helped in Attica. You got to help yourself down there. You know. When we go in, but then we didn't go in. But then we didn't go in.

C: Waited and waited.

D: And when we did go in, I says, "Nobody can help themselves out." They are dead people. And they turned out to be dead but not for the reasons I'm talking about.

C: Yes.

D: Or at least that was in the reports. I don't know.

C: What was it like talking about all this so many years later?

D: I couldn't talk about a lot of it in the beginning for two reasons. Number one, I didn't want to and number two, I couldn't because of the court litigations. Over a period of time I talked to my family. Over a period of time I opened up. My wife knows a lot. I have talked to close associates. What I'm telling you probably has never been told to one person . . .

C: Really?

D: . . . totally. Bits and pieces maybe. Conversations with people. If I talked. Bits and pieces and friends about certain high points that they might understand.

C: Yeah.

D: But the interworkings, the interworkings of the job structure and the thought pattern and have you. They was useless to them. Because you didn't come to me and talk to me about it. I know you are here for a different purpose. But the Department never came up with anything . . .

C: I appreciate your trust.

D: . . . for their training sessions. They never tried to figure the hostages. They never tried to talk to the hostages about it. Auburn wasn't a real riot. Auburn was just a little flea sac. You know. The Korean type thing.

C: Small deal. Attica's the big deal.

D: Attica was the big thing. And they did not follow up after Auburn and I am firmly convinced it should have been.

C: Yeah.

D: They say that this was spontaneous. I say no. I say the same people did it the same way they did it at Auburn. So how the hell can you be spontaneous in that? Maybe it was a spontaneous thing the final trigger, was a spontaneous thing. But then you got to have some kind of a trigger any action is going to be spontaneous if that is the case. But as far as the planning, it was basically done the same way as it was done in Auburn.

C: I've heard other people say that.

D: And now they are in agreement. I have always asked basically who was criminally responsible for Attica. I was asked that question a number of times. I have since then, with the people, so it is not, it is not you know, the criminal stuff is over with. They would say the inmates caught us by surprise. Because that I'm not into death and destruction. They reacted to a situation and they were spontaneous or not spontaneous. Certain things took place. And they say the officers asked for it because they took inmates on and tried to help them or whatever. I says, nah, that was not it either. Attica I hold criminally, who I hold criminally responsible in Attica is ——— and ———. These men had the power at that point in time to control the situation. I will never hold them for their decisions. But when somebody like the Superintendent is trying to get feedback to him about his institution and what he needs and they relegate him to go back to the office as an office boy because they're going to run the show. At that point in time those two men crossed that line, that fine line and they became criminal in their actions. They are criminally responsible for every death in Attica. They didn't listen to the feedback to make a decision.

C: They didn't listen.

D: That, *that* they were supposed to do. This day and age you listen to feedback.

C: Yeah.

D: You get it before you make the decisions. There is time in this business. You bought time. There is a lot of psychology. My approach. My time to think, to get total feedback and base those decisions based on that. Not shell out because you don't want to listen to it. Not to shell out because it is not in your world of thinking. To me ——— was nothing. And after it was over with, maybe years later when I was on the staff and they asked me [what I thought]. The governor had his emissary there. He relied on that emissary [the commissioner] who was feeding him all that information. The State Police as a matter of fact were feeding him [the commissioner] the information. That man effectively stopped the feedback [to the governor] that was necessary to control Attica. He stopped it therefore.

C: He was the Commissioner in charge.

D: In corrections at that time.

C: If, was the Superintendent . . .

D: I watched ———. ——— was the Deputy Commissioner. I think they were both out of California. Imported from outside the State.

C: Yeah.

D: Which didn't set too well with us.

C: Yeah. Yeah.

D: A Commissioner by the name of ——— who had helped put that thing down was drummed out of the business because Auburn happened. ——— wasn't drummed out of the business because of Attica. You know. That's something that not very many people know. What my feelings are aren't exactly why Attica developed and who was criminally responsible for it. What amnesty was granted, no matter what the hell I said at that point. And when amnesty was granted, everything was all over with except to fill out the reports. There was one person and one person . . . you better believe what those type of people in power, their thought processes. You better believe whatever they did after that was wrong. My eyes and a lot of other eyes . . .

C: Right.

D: The follow-up, their help with other people. Whatever. These people weren't giving them any help. Today we didn't have that. Today over the years they have come up with some good people. Today we have the best man in the business. I would follow him to the end of the earth.

C: No kidding . . .

D: The man is a modern-type manager. He's got the brains. Uses total feedback. He surrounds himself with a team of staff. He pays for performance and not lip service. There were no political payoffs in that man. This I like. This is my style. I suppose I will stay a long time. If he leaves, I probably will walk out.

C: Yeah.

D: I have a lot of faith in the Department today.

C: Yeah.

D: I find fault with various bits and pieces which is common.

C: Sure.

D: But the faith, it will never be deterred.

C: Overall.

D: Not, not the way it's being run today. To me, it is being run professionally. Today it is being run with the proper tools needed, to not only accomplish the goal, but also to accomplish within the guidelines of the law, which has become over years it became quite hampered, to say the least.

C: Really.

D: And I know because I, I went and got this thing. I know how to make each in terms of support. It tells you how to handle every kind of trick in the book. Every kind of a, inmate right in the book. They start you off with the rights for witnesses, the rights to know, the rights to be told in advance, the rights to refer a case. All hampering on administration, the function.

C: Yeah.

D: But if you didn't close your mind to it, you could take that system and like a court system.

C: Make it work.

D: Run and run well. And that is what I am doing.

C: Have there ever been any after-effects of your experience that you haven't discussed yet, like flashbacks?

D: No. Never had that problem. The only thing I had that was over that breaking down in the middle of the road across from Attica and crying in my wife's arms like a baby. On my knees with everybody watching. I mean, I cried. I mean, I never had that happen in my life. I did get emotional sometimes when I see something that is like that. And the tears might come. Well, I mean that was a total break-up. That is the only time in my whole life time that I can remember being in that position.

C: How did you feel about having done that?

D: I think that is the reason I went back in to Attica and functioned from this point on. I let it out.

C: Let it out.

D: That is the way I let it out.

C: Kind of let the tension out.

D: Must be that, had been building for some time.

C: Yeah.

D: That had been building for some time. I know of no time where I have ever had nightmares, no problems sleeping from it. I know of no time where it has ever affected my judgement on the job. I had no problems with that. We're talking about personality here. And we're talking about every person is different.

C: Sure.

D: They need. I suppose what they need are trained psychologists. People that can, can take each personality and work with them and I don't mean that the Department should come in and handle 40 people on a caseload. They are going to flood the place with 40 psychologists for 40 people.

C: Sure.

D: And then maybe working without them if they want feedback. I don't know.

C: Work with each individual. Individual support.

D: I would say they definitely should recognize a need of people that need some help. Maybe I was lucky nothing ever happened to me that could have ruined my life because of it. Who knows. History is made because of certain things. But I was, I was strictly helped . . .

C: Yeah.

D: Or I guess my family did suffer a little bit after that because my wife and I sort of went our separate ways. I worked so many long hours; I was so involved in my job. So involved in what I felt was right that I started carrying it home in the wrong way. And my wife and I had just separated just enough, not separated separated, we just sort of separated in our association.

C: Yeah.

D: To a point where it became dangerous to our marriage.

C: Moved you apart a little bit. Did she give you feedback?

D: Over thirty years, over thirty years I came back. I came back better than it was before. Hell, now I am up here on the road all time. I don't go out.

C: Yeah.

D: I have no urge to go out.

C: Yeah.

D: I am home just as much as I am awake. My wife and I have a very good relationship and I trust her and she trusts me. There are no problems.

C: Uh huh.

D: And yet, I'm on the road. I'm, man if I was on the road when this happened back in 1971, 70, 71, 72. Forget it. Our marriage would have gone down the tubes.

C: Yeah.

D: I know that.

C: Yeah.

D: The only reason it held together was because we had been together for so long because, you know, you just couldn't separate.

C: Yeah.

D: Then we got over the rough spot. So that was really the only flashback I have ever had.

C: Did she or others ever tell you that it seemed like it had affected you, changed you?

D: Nobody ever told me that I had changed. Not even my wife.

C: I see.

D: Nobody, nobody ever got into it. Not my mother, who lived down in Florida. Not my wife's folks. I think, they lived in Florida at the time. We were basically on our own.

C: Yeah.

D: The whole family structure. I have very few relatives. I had a few relatives in Auburn. She had no relatives. Maybe that is what happened. We were there together and through thick and thin eventually we are going to have to be the two coming out of it.

C: Kind of pioneer kind of spirit.

D: And we came through it. But without help. I could have lost my marriage. I could have lost me. I could have lost my career. I had no help. The Department is remiss for that part.

C: Uh huh.

D: The follow-up. That was theirs. By the grace of God I suppose, I know.

C: You put the grace of God in there. I think it seemed like it took a lot of determination and courage as well.

D: Whatever.

C: Anything else that I didn't ask about that I should have . . . ?

D: You brought out some things I wouldn't have mentioned on my own. My answers to the question itself. I have a feeling that we have probably much said everything. This is pretty much what you wanted.

C: Okay. You have been very, very, very helpful. I really appreciate it.

D: I have a different perception of Auburn from what ———— would tell you because I guess they used a tactic different than was used to me.

C: Yes.

D: My perception from ———— would be different. He was taken hostage out of the kitchen area. I was taken hostage out the block. I should have been in the kitchen working with him but it was my day off and I had swapped with someone.

C: Hmm.

D: That is something else to think about. That was my day off and I was in there. I had swapped.

C: Your day off.

D: So I was unlucky to be in there. If I had been in my kitchen basement

I am firmly believed I would never been taken hostage because there I control my own destiny.

C: You controlled that.

D: We had gone through a set-to on a Monday afternoon where they were going to take over the yard and everything else. And I had done certain things down in their area to protect the inmates and myself. Certain things I was going to do. Now of course I was up in this strange and hostile place. I was posted at a block that I was not familiar with when I was taken hostage. And my basement was taken. And I felt that it would never have been, had I been down there and had done the same thing I had done Monday afternoon.

C: Yeah.

D: Those were history things.

C: Amazing, isn't it.

D: But it would have happened anyway. It was my day off anyway. I just wouldn't have been taken hostage.

C: Right.

D: I had swapped. I do know that I was going to college at the time and Tuesday was election day and I did go up to my evening courses at the college. I did have some guys that were in the courses with me that were from the prison and one guy's name was ———, a Lieutenant in Auburn now. I says, "What is it like in there?" He says, "The place is going to tip over tomorrow." Well, I had my mind set that it was going to tip over like it did Monday. Right? Why? I went in to work with the thought that, hmm, the place is going to tip over! We opened up that morning and of course I was the second officer in the block and I went up to get the keys behind the officers and one thing did take place. Came out of those galleries and that was really out of the ordinary stuff. And then they of course after that point, certain things took place that I suppose were administrative decisions but whether I agree with them or not. Or what actions I took. Or what action I finally took. They took these inmates. And that's that. That is where administration . . . something had to do with psychology . . .

C: Yeah.

D: . . . at that point. The hostage-taking was, you know, two hours later. And you know. You'd have to talk. That was the beginning. That was the pioneer stage. Having a problem, which you have to do is associate that day would be bring in what they are doing today on another level, what they would do for the after-effects of the day or their approach to it. What their intervention teams are taught to do and things like that.

C: Yeah.

D: Other than that, I don't know if I got that much more.

C: Okay. Thank you again.

DICTATED FIELD NOTES AFTER INTERVIEW WITH DAVID

That is the end of the taped interview with Lieutenant ———. After the tape machine was turned off he was eager to talk further and probably stayed with me another half hour. During this time he shared with me that I was the first person that he had ever shared all that information with in such a comprehensive way.

He seemed truly to develop a rapport with me and spoke about stopping in to see me on Cape Cod if he was ever out that way. He talked about it as if he really would have liked to do that. He invited me to come up to Watertown during the day for a tour if I liked. He was very friendly.

He became visibly moved during parts of the interview, especially when describing seeing his wife after the retaking of Attica prison. His use of language was interesting in that he seemed to be trying to use words to make himself sound very sophisticated or educated. It didn't come across in a way that seemed ingenuous or pompous, but perhaps a bit insecure. He made it a point to talk about his academic training and that he was so close to finishing his Bachelor's Degree.

He came across as very personable, fully genuine and authentic. He was very up front in letting me know that there were certain things he would not talk about, although it seemed like he crossed that line a few times in the flow and intensity of the conversation.

His living quarters were rather spartan to say the least. He's living with three other men in very small, second floor of a rural, wooden apartment house with two men to a room. The rooms were divided by unfinished plywood. Furniture was very battered and old. For all four of these men, these are just temporary quarters while they are, as they put it, "on the road." Their families and homes are elsewhere in the State.

Part of Lieutenant ———'s willingness to speak freely to me, I think, comes from his security in being able to retire tomorrow if he wished, although he has no plans to. As he mentioned to me at the end of the interview, if I were to go to the newspapers with the material tomorrow, he could simply retire if he was getting any flack. He seems to take great pride in his professionalism and the growing professionalism of the Department and in the leadership of the Department of Correctional Services. He said that he would follow ———, the Commissioner, "to the ends of the earth."

The theme that seemed to come across again and again in the conversation, that will probably come out in the transcript, but was emphasized in his non-verbals, was the theme of control. Being in control and taking control of situations involving his job and involving inmates in prisons, was crucial to him. One can speculate that being put right back into the job of taking control again immediately after being released as a hostage, perhaps was helpful to him in that he was put back in control. Although not planned, it might be comparable to the treatment for combat soldiers who are briefly treated for combat fatigue and combat stress and then put back into the front lines.

For Lieutenant ———, this may have been therapeutic. It was at Attica where four days of waiting, four days of helplessness, left him feeling at the end of his rope. Such that the climax, the release of tension after the waiting, after the takeover, after the horror of seeing the carnage in the yard and all the dead and the dying—it all came out in the middle of the street. It was the very poignant scene of meeting his wife. He ran across to her in the middle of the road and fell down on his knees and sobbed on her lap.

It is worth noting that during each of the interviews there appears to be that kind of scene. A poignant, moving scene that seems to be climatic and a release of tension. For some, it came immediately upon release when they realized that they were free. For others, it seemed like it came at other moments.

The anger at the Department that other hostages have spoken of appears to be present with Lieutenant ——— as well. His anger at Administration, at the Auburn and Attica facilities as well as the central office in Albany is profound. He no longer feels that anger. He feels the Department has transformed itself. It has new leadership, professional leadership. He feels that the present administration listens to the people who are the source. Listening, for him, is key. He noted that at Auburn and Attica they were not paying attention to the people, to the men who knew what was going on. In his own work he stressed the importance of listening to the professionals, not using the rat system of inmates ratting on others but relying on professionals to use professional observation and judgment to determine what is going on within a facility. Listening, for him, is extremely important. In just listening to him, I encouraged him to release a great deal of information, a lot more than he had planned to talk about when we sat down.

It is very much worth noting the profound effect that a hostage experience has on these men many years, 16 or 17 years, later. These men, in talking about these experiences, their faces become flushed or white. Their eyes become heavy and tearful. They, at times, are on the verge of crying, become choked up in describing different moments, different events, different thoughts.

It is also fascinating to note that they, the men who were at the same incident, for instance various men at Auburn, described the experience from profoundly different perspectives. Others besides Lieutenant —— —— have described the experience very differently. It is as if you become extremely subjective during the intensity of that moment and become very much tuned in to what is happening to you and what is happening immediately around you. This is probably a useful survival skill. Lieutenant —— also described, in the same way as Lieutenant —— at Elmira, of becoming somewhat hyperalert, hypervigilant, mind racing, thinking about strategic ways to cope, ways to save your life, determining many courses of action and instantly analyzing them. He found himself considering many choices with lightning speed.

It is also interesting to note that Lieutenant —— described several things about other subjects whom I had interviewed. He described —— —— in the category of someone who was not profoundly affected and was able to go back to work, progress within the Department and retire as a senior officer. When I talked to ——, it became apparent that he was profoundly affected by the experience. He had been hospitalized. He had been abusing alcohol and valium and came close to suicide. He had left the Department for a while before returning to it. It affected him very deeply.

I observed how often Lieutenant —— described things in terms of their structure. He must have used the word structure a great number of times. It seems that it was part of his coping mechanisms to rely on the structure, the chain of command. The training, the professionalism, the uniform, all those things were part of his way of coping. He threw himself into the job perhaps as a way of coping with the after-effects of the experience. He was somewhat vague, even when pressed, in describing the effects on his personal life, his marriage and personal relationships.

He said, only in a general way, that it had a profound effect and led him close to a divorce. He and his wife had "worked it through," however, and he felt his marriage was strong because of the challenge and the testing. He also described himself as having benefitted from the experience. He had some of his ideas confirmed and his self-reliance tested and proven strong. He seemed to take great pride in that.

While I have not seen much evidence of a formal development of the Stockholm Syndrome in the usual sense, I have heard some things that might be relevant to that dynamic.

Lieutenant ————, as well as other officers, former hostages whom I have interviewed such as ———— at Elmira, ———— and others have talked about how certain inmates helped them, protected them, encouraged them, offered them assistance or medical care. There was some differentiation in their mind between the "good inmates" and "bad inmates." In their view, there was a very important difference between the minority of inmates who planned and executed the riot and the vast majority of inmates who really wanted nothing to do with it. They have felt very grateful to the few inmates who showed them some caring and support during the incident. A survivor of the Attica riot went to some lengths to report the inmates who gave him assistance and saw to it that those inmates were offered some reward for their efforts.

The other quality of the Stockholm Syndrome, attitude change toward authority, is certainly there. The hostages, during and after the event, very consistently, perhaps accurately, it is hard to know, described the actions of those in authority with anger and contempt. ———— spoke about feeling "Where the hell are they? Why aren't they coming in here to get me out?" There was anger about mismanagement, anger at feeling the authorities did not listen to the people on the front line, anger because of mismanagement of the negotiations, mismanagement of the media, mismanagement of contact with family members. ———— spoke of afterwards people giving him the feedback that he was an angry man.

Lieutenant ———— spoke about himself as a maverick. Someone who is willing to stand apart and take chances, take risks. He seemed to regard some of the other hostage survivors similarly. He respected the people who went back in to the "bowels of the institution." For him, they had a special kind of courage.

Lieutenant ———— described how he felt that, while there may be other hostage-takings at other institutions or even at his own institution, it will never occur immediately around him or in an area that he has some direct control over. He felt extremely confident in his ability to prevent that from happening and seemed to explain the hostage incident at Auburn, and his being taken there, because he was not in his own element. He was not in the kitchen. He had swapped with someone else. He was covering a different area that was not his usual domain.

There appears to be some fairly universal anger among the former hostages toward the Department in that they felt uncared for, and disregarded after their traumatic experience. Lieutenant ———— spoke of the chaplain who called his wife with a cursory message saying that her husband had been taken hostage and they didn't know anything about his condition and then hanging up, leaving his wife and children rather traumatized by the message and their speculation about his status.

There was no regard for the men having been through a traumatic experience and needing some interviewing, debriefing, support, medical attention or observation in the moments, hours, days and weeks after the event. There was no perceived follow-up with family or with hostages. Lieutenant ———— was the only one so far to say that there was a written survey sent around—a questionnaire asking for some feedback about certain things. It seemed more focused on the strategic management of the situation such as, "Would you have wanted us to go in and get you right away even if it meant taking more chances and risks?" Those kinds of questions, not on, "How did you do after you were released? How was your family? What could we have done for you? Did you need time off?"—those kinds of things. After Attica there was a bit more follow-up and the people were automatically given a leave. It was acknowledged as a more traumatic experience. There was national attention, people killed, and scenes of brutal carnage.

Auburn was undervalued as a traumatic and important experience for the men involved, the men who were taken hostage as well as the men who were not taken hostage. That is one theme that was also coming through as I talk to people. Even people who were not hostages but involved in the periphery of these events have suffered some after-effects. That has not been the focus of this study, but it could be valuable to consider in the future. The hostages described, at times with some anger and resentment, that people who were not even taken hostage couldn't go back to work or were very shaken up. They couldn't function after the event. "You weren't even a hostage and I'm back to work. Why aren't you back to work? Nothing happened to you."

Lieutenant ————, having experienced this trauma uniquely from both perspectives, makes it very clear that being on the outside, the feeling of not knowing, the helplessness, the uncertainty, the continuously being on alert, hypervigilant, also takes a toll. The identification with the brother officer inside is intense. The feeling of, "It could be me," is very much a part of their experience. There may even be a certain guilt of, "Why not me?"

Some broad-based debriefing and management of officers after an incident would seem to be indicated. Not only the hostages need attention. There needs to be some debriefing, at least, with men who served in support functions, such as an intervention team or a negotiation team. One hostage told the story about a negotiator who, after the Sing-Sing negotiation that lasted for days, constantly on edge, constantly vigilant, went out to a motel and got drunk for several days as his own way of de-stressing. It seems clear that all the people involved in such an intense situation need some support afterwards. All were affected in profound ways. Their families were affected in profound ways. There needs to be some acknowledgement of that and some support provided.

References

Abrahamsen, D. (1973). *The Murdering Mind.* New York: Harper & Row.

American Psychiatric Association. (1987). *Diagnostic and Statistical Manual* (3rd ed. revised). Washington, D.C.: Author.

American Psychological Association. (1982). *Ethical Principles in the Conduct of Research With Human Participants.* Washington, D.C.: Author.

American Psychological Association. (1984). *Final Report.* American Psychological Association Task Force on the Victims of Crime and Violence. Washington, D.C.: Author.

Bandura, A. (1977). Self-efficacy towards a unifying theory of behavioral change. *Psychological Review,* 84, 191–215.

Bard, M. and Sangrey, D. (1986). *The Crime Victim's Book.* (2nd ed.) New York: Brunner/Mazel, Inc.

————. (1980). Things fall apart: Victims in crisis. *Evaluation and Change,* 28-35.

Belz, M., Parker, E. Z., Sank, L. I., Shaffer, C., Shapiro, J. Shriber, L. (1977). Is there a treatment for terror? *Psychology Today,* October, 54-56, 1108-1112.

Bettelheim, B. (1980). *Surviving and Other Essays.* New York: Vintage Books.

Biklen, S. K. (1973). *Lessons of Consequences: Women's Perception of their Elementary School Experiences, A Retrospective Study.* University of Massachusetts: Unpublished Doctoral Dissertation.

Blumer, H. (1969). *Symbolic Interactionism.* Englewood Cliffs, N.J.: Prentice Hall.

Bogdan, R. C. and Taylor, S. J. (1975). *Introduction to Qualitative Research*

Methods. New York: John Wiley and Sons, Inc.

Bodgan, R. C. and Biklen, S. K. (1982). *Qualitative Research for Education: An Introduction to Theory and Methods*. Boston: Allyn and Bacon.

Borg, W. R. and Gall, M. D. (1983). *Educational Research: An Introduction*. New York: Longna Inc.

Bulman, R. I. and Wortman, C. B. (1977). Attributions of blame and coping in the "real world": Severe accident victims react to their lot. *Journal of Personality and Social Psychology*, 35, 351-363.

Burgess, A. W. and Holmstrom, L. L. (1974). Rape trauma syndrome. *American Journal of Psychiatry*, 131, 981–986.

Caplan, G. (1974). Support systems and community mental health. New York: Behavioral Publications.

Chelimisky, E. (1980). Serving victims: Agency incentives and individuals' needs. In S. E. Salasin (Ed.), *Evaluating Victim Services*. Beverly Hills, California: Sage.

Coates, D., and Winston, T. (1983). Counteracting the disease of depression. *Journal of Social Issues*, 39, 171-196.

Coates, D., Wortman, C. B., and Abbey, A. (1979). Reaction to victims. In I. H. Frieze, D. Bar-Tal, and J. S. Carroll (Eds.), *New Approaches to Social Problems: Applications of Attribution Theory*. San Francisco: Jossey Bass.

Cobb, S. (1976). Social support as a moderator of life stress. *Psychosomatic Medicine*, 38, 300-314.

Dean, A., and Lin, N. (1977). The stress buffering role of social support. *Journal of Nervous and Mental Disease*, 165, 403-417.

Dor-Shav, N. K. (1978). On the long-range effects of concentration camp internment on Nazi victims: 25 years later. *Journal of Consulting Psychology*, 446, 1-11.

Eitinger, L. (1982). The effects of captivity. In Ochberg, F. M. and Soskis, D. A. (Eds.) *Victims of Terrorism*. Boulder, Colorado: Westview Press, Inc.

Epstein, S. (1973). The self-concept revisited: Or a theory of a theory. *American Psychologist*, 28, 404–416.

Epstein, S. (1980). The self-concept: A review and the proposal of an integrated theory of personality. In E. Staub (Ed.), *Personality: Basic Issues and Current Research*. Englewood Cliffs, N.J.: Prentice Hall.

Everstine, D. S. and Everstine, L. (1983). *People in Crisis: Strategic Therapeutic Interventions*. New York: Brunner/Mazel.

Fattah, E. A. (1979). Some reflections on the victimology of terrorism. *Terrorism: An International Journal*, 3, 81-108.

Fenyvesi, C. (1977). Living with a fearful memory. *Psychology Today*. October, 61, 115-116.

Fields, R. M. (1980). *Victims of Terrorism: The Effects of Prolonged Stress*. *Evaluation and Change*. Special issue.

Figley, C. R. (1985). From victim to survivor: Social responsibility in the wake of catastrophe. In Figley, C. R. (Ed.), *Trauma and Its Wake: The Study and Treatment of Post-Traumatic Stress Disorder.* New York: Brunner/Mazel, Inc.

Figley, C. R., Sprenkle, D. H. (1978). Delayed stress response syndrome: Family therapy indication. *Journal of Marriage and Family Counseling, 4,* 53-60.

Flannery, R. B. (1986). Personal control as a moderator variable of life stress: Preliminary inquiry. *Psychological Reports, 55,* 200-202.

———. (1987). From victim to survivor: A stress management approach in the treatment of learned helplessness. In B. A. VanDer Kolk, Ed. *Psychological Trauma.* Washington, D.C.: American Psychiatric Press.

Frankl, V. E. (1969). *Man's Search for Meaning: An Introduction to Logotherapy.* New York: Washington Square Press.

Frederick, C. J. (1980). Effects of natural vs. human-induced violence upon victims. *Evaluation and Change.* (Spring), 71-75.

Frederick, C. J. (1981). Aircraft accident: Emergency mental health problems. Rockville, Maryland: National Institute of Mental Health.

Freud, A. (1974). *The Ego and the Mechanisms of Defense.* New York: International University Press.

Freud, S. (1920). *Beyond the Pleasure Principle.* In Strachey, J. (Ed.) (1955) *The Standard Edition of the Complete Psychological Works of Sigmund Freud.* London: Hogarth Press.

———. (1926). Inhibitions, symptoms and anxiety. In *The Complete Psychological Works,* standard ed., 30. Translated and edited by J. Strachey. London: Hogarth Press, 1959, 75-175.

Friedman, K., Bischoff, H., Davis, R. C., and Person, A. (1982). Victims and helpers: Reactions to crime. New York: Victims Service Agency.

Glaser, B. C. and Strauss, A. L. (1967). *The Discovery of Grounded Theory: Strategies for Qualitative Research.* New York: Aldine Publishing Co.

Gottlieb, B. H. (1979). The primary group as supportive milieu: Applications to community psychology. *American Journal of Community Psychology, 7,* 469-489.

Green, A. H. (1983). Dimensions of psychological trauma in abused children. *Journal of the American Association of Child Psychiatry.* 22, 231-237.

Grinker, R. R. and Spiegel, J. P. (1944), Brief psychotherapy in war neuroses. *Psychosomatic Medicine, 6.*

Hartsough, D. M. (1988). Traumatic stress as an area for research. *Journal of Traumatic Stress,* 1(22), 145–154.

Hauben, R. (1983). Hostage taking: The Dutch Experience. In L. Z. Freedman and Y. Alexander (Eds.). *Perspectives on Terrorism.* Wilmington, Delaware: Scholarly Resources, Inc.

Haward, L. R. (1960). The subjective meaning of stress. *British Journal of*

Medical Psychology, 33, 185-194.

Hillman, R. G. (1981). The psychopathology of being held hostage. *American Journal of Psychiatry*, 138, 9, 1193–1197.

Hirsch, B. J. (1980). Natural support systems and coping with major life changes. *American Journal of Community Psychology*, 8, 159-172.

Janoff-Bulman, R. (1982). Esteem and central bases of blame: "Adaptive" strategies for victims versus observers. *Journals of Personality*, 50, 180-192.

Janoff-Bulman, R. and Frieze, I. H. (1982). A theoretical perspective for understanding reactions to victimization. *Journal of Social Issues*, 39, 2, 1-17.

————. (1983). A theoretical perspective for understanding reactions to victimization. *Journal of Social Issues*, 39, 2, 1-18.

Jenkins, B. M. (1976). Hostage survival: Some preliminary observations. Rand Corporation Report, P-5627.

Johnson, J. H. and Savason, I. G. (1978). Life stress, depression and anxiety: Internal-external control as a moderator variable. *Journal of Psychosomatic Research*, 22, 205-208.

Kilpatrick D. G., Resick, P. A. and Veronen, L. J. (1981). Effects of a rape experience: A longitudinal study. *Journal of Social Issue*, 37, 4, 105-122.

Kiresuk, T. J. and Lund S. (1981). Knowledge transfer for victim services. In S. B. Salasin (Ed.), *Evaluating Victim Services*. Beverly Hills, California: Sage.

Kutash, I. (1978). Treating the victim of aggression. In I. Kutash and L. Schlesinger (Eds.), *Violence: Perspective on Murder and Aggression*. San Francisco: Jossey Bass.

Lazarus, R. S., Averill, J. R. and Opton, E. M. (1974). The psychology of coping: Issue of research and assessment. In G. V. Coelho, O. A. Hamburg, and J. E. Adams (Eds.), *Coping and Adaptation*. New York: Basic Books.

Lazarus, R. S. and Launier, R. (1978). Stress-related transactions between person and environment. In L. A. Pervin and M. Lewis (Eds.), *Perspectives in International Psychology*. New York: Plenum.

Lerner, J. J. (1980). *The Belief in a Just World*. New York: Plenum Press.

Lerner, M. (1970). The desire for justice and reactions to victims: Social psychological studies of antecedents and consequences. In J. Macaulay and L. Berkowitz (Eds.), *Altruism and Helping Behavior*. New York: Academic Press.

Lidz, T. (1946). Psychiatric casualties from Guadacanal: A study of reactions to extreme stress. *Psychiatry*, 9, 193-215.

Lifton, R. J. (1967). *Death in Life: Survivors of Hiroshima*. New York: Simon and Schuster.

————. (1976). *The Life of the Self*. New York: Simon and Schuster.

————. (1983). *The Broken Connection*. New York: Basic Books.

Lindy, J. D., Green, B. L., Grace, M., and Titchener, J. (1983). *American Journal of Psychotherapy*, 37(4), 593-610.

Luker, Kristin (1976). *Taking Changes*. Berkeley: University of California Press.

Maddi, S. R. and Kobasa, S. C. (1984). The hardy executive: health under stress. Homewood, Illinois: Dow Jones–Irwin.

Mead, G. H. (1934). *Mind, Self and Society*. Chicago: University of Chicago.

Meltzer, B. and Petras, J. W. (1970). The Chicago and Iowa schools of symbolic interactionism. In Shibutani, T. (Ed.) *Human Nature and Collective Behavior: Papers in Honor of Herbert Blumer*. Englewood Cliffs, N.J.: Prentice-Hall, Inc.

Merbaum, M. and Hefez, A. (1976). Some personality characteristics of soldiers exposed to extreme war stress. *Journal of Consulting and Clinical Psychology*, 44, 1-6.

Monat, A. and Lazarus, R. S. (1977). *Stress and Coping: An Anthology*. New York: Columbia University Press.

Morris, P. (1975). *Loss and Change*. Garden City, N.J.: Anchor/Doubleday.

Niederland, W. (1968). Clinical observations on the "Survivor Syndrome." *International Journal of Psychoanalysis*, 49, 313-315.

Ochberg, F. (1978). The victim of terrorism: Psychiatric considerations. *Terrorism: An International Journal*, 1, 147-168.

Ochberg, F. M., and Soskis, D. A. (1982). *Victims of Terrorism*. Boulder, Co.: Westview Press.

Parkes, C. M. (1971). Psycho-social transitions: A field for study. *Social Science and Medicine*, 5, 101-115.

Parkes, C. (1975). Unexpected and untimely bereavement: A statistical study of young Boston widows and widowers. In B. Schoenberg et. al (Eds.), *Bereavement: Its Psychological Aspects*. New York: Columbia University Press, 119-138.

Parson, E. R. (1990). Post-Traumatic Demoralization Syndrome (PTDS). *Journal of Contemporary Psychotherapy*, 20(1) 17-33.

Pennebaker, J. W. (1985). Traumatic experience and psychosomatic disease: Exploring the roles of behavioral inhibition, obsession, and confiding. *Canadian Psychology*, 26, 82-95.

Petersen, A. C. and Spiga, R. (1982) Adolescence and stress. In Goldberger, L. and Breznitz, S. (Eds.) *Handbook of Stress: Theoretical and Clinical Aspects*. New York: Free Press.

President's Task Force on Victims of Crime: Final Report. (1982). Washington, D.C.: U.S. Government Printing Office.

Rahe, R. H., and Genender, C. (1983). Adaptation to recovery from captivity stress. *Military Medicine*, 148, 577–585.

Rahe, R. H., Karson, S., Howard, N. S., Rubin, R. T. and Poland, R. E. (1990). Psychological and physiological assessments on American hostages freed from captivity in Iran. *Psychosomatic Medicine,* 52, 1-16.

Reissman, F. (1965). The "helper therapy" principle. *Social Work.* 10, 27-32.

Rich, R., and Stenzel, S. (1980). Mental health services for victims: Policy paradigms. *Evaluation and Change,* Special issues, 47-54.

Rieff, R. (1979). *The Invisible Victim: The Criminal Justice System's Forgotten Responsibility.* New York: Basic Books.

Rogers, C. R. (1961). *On Becoming a Person.* Boston: Houghton Mifflin.

Ryan, W. (1971). *Blaming the Victim.* New York: Vintage Books.

Salasin, S. E. (Ed.). (1981). *Evaluating Victim Services.* Beverly Hills, California: Sage.

Sales, E., Baum, M. and Shore, B. (1984). Victim readjustment following assault. *Journal of Social Issues,* 40(1), 117-136.

Segal, J., Hunter, E. J., and Segal, Z. (1976). Universal consequences of captivity: Stress reactions among divergent populations of prisoners of war and their families. *International Social Science Journal,* 28, 593-609.

Segal, J. (1986). *Winning Life's Toughest Battles.* New York: McGraw-Hill.

Seligman, M.(ed.) (1975). *Helplessness: On Depression, Development and Death.* San Francisco: Freeman.

Sharfstein, S. (1980). Caring for victims: An interview by Susan Salasin. *Evaluation and Change,* Special issue, 18-20.

Shore, J. H. (1986). *Disaster Stress Studies: New Methods and Findings.* Washington, D.C.: American Psychiatric Press.

Siegel, M. (1983). Crime and violence in America. *American Psychologist,* 38, 1267-1273.

Siegel, R. K. (1984). Hostage hallucinations: Visual imagery induced by isolation and life-threatening stress. *Journal of Nervous and Mental Disease,* 172 (5), 264-271.

Silver, R. L., Boon, C. and Stones, M. H. (1983). Searching for meaning in misfortune: Making sense of incest. *Journal of Social Issues,* 39(2), 81-102.

Silver, R. L., and Wortman, C. B. (1980). Coping with undesirable life events. In J. Garber and M. E. Seligman (Eds.), *Human Helplessness.* New York: Academic Press.

Silver, R., Wortman, C. B., and Kos, D. (1982). Cognitive, affective, and coping responses: New directions for human helplessness research. *Journal of Personality,* 50(4), 396-429.

Simon, R. I. and Blum, R. A. (1987). After the terrorist incident: Psychotherapeutic treatments of former hostages. *American Journal of Psychotherapy,* 16, (2), 194-200.

Sledge, W. H., Boydstun, J. A., and Rahe, A. J. (1980). Self concept changes related to war captivity. *Archives of General Psychiatry,* 37, 430-443.

Spiegel, D. (1988). Dissociation and hypnosis in post-traumatic stress disorders. *Journal of Traumatic Stress.* 1(1) 17-33.

Strentz, T. (1982). The Stockholm Syndrome: Law enforcement policy and hostage behavior. In F. M. Ochberg and D. A. Soskis (Eds.), *Victims of Terrorism.* Boulder, Co.: Westview Press.

Swank, R. L. (1949). Combat exhaustion: A descriptive and statistical analysis of causes, symptoms and signs. *Journal of Nervous and Mental Diseases,* 109, 475-508.

Symonds, M. (1980). The second injury to victims. *Evaluation and Change.* Special issue, 36-38.

Terr, L. C. (1981). Psychic trauma in children. Observation following the Chowchilla school bus kidnapping. *American Journal of Psychiatry,* 138, 1, 14-19.

———. (1983). Chowchilla revisited: The effects of the psychic trauma four years after a school bus kidnapping. *American Journal of Psychiatry,* 140, 1543-1550.

Thomas, W. I. (1928). *The Unadjusted Girl.* Boston: Little, Brown, Inc.

Thompson, S. C. (1985). Finding positive meaning in a stressful event and coping. *Basic and Applied Social Psychology,* 6(4), 279-295.

Ursano, R. J. (1981). The Viet Nam era prisoner of war: Precaptivity personality and the development of psychiatric illness. *American Journal of Psychiatry,* 138, 315-318.

U.S. Department of Justice. (1979). Criminal victimization in the United States: Summary findings on 1977-1978. Washington, D.C.: U.S. Government Printing Office.

Vaillant, G. F. and Vaillant, C. (1981). National history of male psychological health, X: Work as a predictor of positive mental health. *American Journal of Psychiatry,* 138, 1433-1440.

Van der Ploeg, H. M., and Kleijn, W. C. (1989). Being held hostage in the Netherlands: A study of long-term aftereffects. *Journal of Traumatic Stress,* 2(2), 153-169.

Weis, K., and Weis, S. (1975). Victimology and the justification of rape. In I. Drapkin and E. Viano (Eds.), *Victimology: A New Focus,* Lexington, MA: Lexington Books.

Wesselius, C. L., and DeSarno, J. V. (1983). The anatomy of a hostage situation. *Behavioral Science and the Law,* 1, 2, 33-45.

Wortman, C. B. (1983). Coping with victimization: conclusions and implications for future research. *Journal of Social Issues,* 39(2), 195-221.

Wortman, C. B., Abbey, A., Holland, A. E., Silver, R. L., and Janoff-Bulman, R. (1980). Transitions from the laboratory to the field: Problems and progress. In L. Bickman (Ed.), *Applied Social Psychology Annual.* Beverly Hills, Ca.: Sage Publications.

Yalom, I. D. (1980). *Existential Psychotherapy*. New York: Basic Books.

Zimbardo, P. G., Haney, C., Banks, W. C., and Jaffe, D., (1975). The psychology of imprisonment: Privation, power, and pathology. In D. Rosenhan and P. London (Eds.), *Theory and Research in Abnormal Psychology*, (3rd ed.). New York: Holt, Rinehart and Winston, 270-287.

Index

About the Author

JAMES F. CAMPBELL is a staff psychologist in the Counseling Center at the University of Rhode Island and an adjunct professor in the Department of Human Development, Counseling, and Family Studies.